SODA SHOP SALVATION

SODA SHOP
Salvation

RECIPES AND STORIES FROM THE
SWEETER SIDE OF PROHIBITION

RAE KATHERINE EIGHMEY

Minnesota Historical Society Press

Image page 120 from La Guardia and Wagner
Archives, La Guardia Community College / The City
University of New York. All other photographs from
Minnesota Historical Society collections.

www.mhspress.org

The Minnesota Historical Society Press is a member
of the Association of American University Presses.

Manufactured in the United States of America

10 9 8 7 6 5 4 3 2 1

⊗ The paper used in this publication meets the
minimum requirements of the American National
Standard for Information Sciences—Permanence
for Printed Library Materials, ANSI Z39.48-1984.

International Standard Book Number
ISBN: 978-0-87351-908-3 (paper)

Library of Congress Cataloging-in-Publication Data
Eighmey, Rae Katherine.
    Soda shop salvation : recipes and stories from
    the sweeter side of Prohibition / Rae Katherine
    Eighmey.
        pages cm
    Summary: "More than 125 recipes for imagina-
    tive drinks, sundae varieties, and luncheonette
    delights from the 1920s evoke the time of speak-
    easies, newfangled devices, and racy automobiles.
    Tidbits of the history of suffragists and flappers,
    bootleggers and G-men interweave with the reci-
    pes." —Provided by publisher.
Includes bibliographical references and index.
    ISBN 978-0-87351-908-3 (pbk. : alk. paper)
    1. Ice cream, ices, etc. 2. Soft drinks. 3. Sundaes.
    4. Soda fountains—United States—History—
    20th century. 5. Prohibition—United States—
    History—20th century. 6. Luncheons. I. Title.
    II. Title: Recipes and stories from the sweeter
    side of Prohibition.
TX795.E36 2013
641.2—dc23
                                        2013017721

A rousing cheer to those
Who raise their glasses high
Without benefit of booze.

And with thanks to my dad,
Who agreed that sometimes
ice cream
was just fine for breakfast

CONTENTS

Eighteenth Amendment to the Constitution of the United States

Section 1. After one year from the ratification of this article the manufacture, sale, or transportation of intoxicating liquors within, the importation thereof into, or the exportation thereof from the United States and all territory subject to the jurisdiction thereof for beverage purposes is hereby prohibited.

Section 2. The Congress and the several States shall have concurrent power to enforce this article by appropriate legislation.

Section 3. This article shall be inoperative unless it shall have been ratified as an amendment to the Constitution by the legislatures of the several States, as provided in the Constitution, within seven years from the date of the submission hereof to the States by the Congress.

Twenty-first Amendment to the Constitution of the United States

Section 1. The eighteenth article of amendment to the Constitution of the United States is hereby repealed.

Section 2. The transportation or importation into any State, Territory or possession of the United States for delivery or use therein of intoxicating liquors, in violation of the laws thereof, is hereby prohibited.

Section 3. The article shall be inoperative unless it shall have been ratified as an amendment to the Constitution by conventions in the several States, as provided in the Constitution, within seven years from the date of submission hereof to the States by the Congress.

PROHIBITION TIMELINE

April 4, 1917	United States enters World War I
August 1, 1917	Senate passes Eighteenth Amendment, voting 65 to 20
August 10, 1917	World War I Food and Fuel Act controls production of "distilled spirits" made from any product that could be used for food
September 10, 1917	Distribution of liquor stops under war powers
December 8, 1917	President Wilson proclaims that breweries are limited to 70 percent of previous year's grain supply and alcoholic content of beer is limited to 2¾ percent
December 17, 1917	House passes revised Eighteenth Amendment, voting 282 to 128
December 18, 1917	Senate passes revised Eighteenth Amendment, voting 47 to 8
November 11, 1918	United States signs armistice with Germany, ending World War I
November 18, 1918	Congress passes temporary War Prohibition Act
January 16, 1919	Nebraska is the thirty-sixth state to ratify the Eighteenth Amendment, making it part of the Constitution
June 27, 1919	Andrew Volstead introduces H.R. 6810, the Prohibition enforcement act, in the House
July 1919	Wartime Prohibition takes effect
July 22, 1919	Prohibition enforcement act, later called the "Volstead Act," passes the House, 287 to 100

September 5, 1919	Enforcement act passes the Senate with amendment by voice vote
October 6, 1919	Joint congressional conference committee brings forward revised enforcement act
October 8, 1919	Conference committee's Volstead Act adopted without discussion by Senate
October 10, 1919	Conference committee's Volstead Act passes House, 321 to 70
October 27, 1919	Volstead Act vetoed by President Wilson
October 27, 1919	Wilson's veto overridden by House, 176 to 55
October 28, 1919	Wilson's veto overridden by Senate, 65 to 20
January 17, 1920	National Prohibition begins
November 1920	Andrew Volstead reelected
November 1922	Volstead defeated for reelection
February 14, 1933	Twenty-First Amendment, repealing the Eighteenth Amendment, passes Senate, 63 to 22
February 16, 1933	Twenty-First Amendment passes House, 289 to 121
March 22, 1933	President Roosevelt signs Cullen-Harrison Act, allowing manufacture of 3.2 percent beer and light wine
April 7, 1933	Cullen-Harrison Act becomes law
December 5, 1933	Twenty-First Amendment ratified, allowing sale of complete range of alcoholic beverages except in those states that have voted to remain dry

SODA SHOP SALVATION

INTRODUCTION

PROHIBITION CHANGED MORE THAN Americans' drinking habits. It altered the streetscapes of small towns and cities. It helped struggling merchants attract customers with newly devised "dry" beverages. And it significantly increased the nation's consumption of ice cream. These changes and more took place in the familiar space of the local soda fountain.

In the years before World War I, the neighborhood soda shop was the antithesis of the corner saloon. Where the saloon was shuttered and dark, the soda shop's display windows enticed customers. The saloon catered to men, while in the soda shop everyone was welcome. Popular songs and political cartoons showed the saloon siphoning working men's money away from their families; the soda shop offered a glass full of refreshment or an ice cream cone for one thin dime.

When Prohibition arrived following passage and ratification of the Eighteenth Amendment, soda shops expanded their presence and influence. They became the salvation for main streets, liquor-deprived citizens, and even breweries. People flocked to soda fountains set up in pharmacies or as freestanding businesses. The number of successful soda fountains increased dramatically.

Soda fountain trade magazines featured ideas and directions for concocting ice cream desserts and special treats for afternoon or evening refreshments. These publications also offered up suggestions for ice cream in salads and even for breakfast.

Everyday life changed on small-town Main Street and on big-city Broadway as the carefree atmosphere of the soda fountain luncheonette counter encouraged a banker wanting a quick lunch to sit next to a beautician seeking respite or a homemaker with her children out for a treat.

Names from soda shop menus hint at the dimensions of change in this dynamic era: the 1921 Highball, Flapper Frappé, Suffragist, Soldier Boy Kiss, and "Reel" Nice Movie Sundae are among scores of innovative, topical treats that reflect the shifting national experience. In short, the soda shop story offers a cross section of the nation and a window during which to examine the whole Prohibition experience during two decades of dynamic changes and transforming "firsts."

Homeowners installed electricity and telephones. Entertainment became a nationally shared experience as radios broadcast networked programming from coast to coast. Motion pictures, and then movies that talked, brought comedies, dramas, and newsreel scenes from around the world to local theaters.

Women won the right to vote in state and federal elections in 1920, and they began working outside the home in expanded numbers, filling roles beyond classrooms and hospitals, stepping into the nation's offices, and entering into some professions traditionally held only by men. In 1921 President Warren G. Harding even appointed Mabel Walker Willebrandt as U.S. assistant attorney general in charge of Prohibition enforcement.

The United States became a nation on the move. More than a million soldiers returned from the war-torn trenches of France and the celebratory streets of Paris. With peace at hand, people set off across the country, driving their basic black Model T or a stylish roadster manufactured by Buick, Chevrolet, Crossley, Dodge, Nash, Studebaker, or one of dozens of other car innovators.

The country's civic and political positions moved, too. Six constitutional amendments were enacted in the space of twenty years during the tumultuous teens and Roaring Twenties. It is important to consider just how astounding this is: only twenty-seven amendments have been ratified in the entire history of the nation, and nearly a quarter of them were enacted in that short period. Just what significant changes did these amendments bring? They changed American law, politics, and culture by authorizing the federal income tax and direct, public election of U.S. senators. The inauguration date for president, vice president, and the new congressional term was advanced to January from March, eliminating four months of lame-duck government. Woman suffrage was approved, and, of course, Prohibition was enacted and then repealed.

Little wonder people in small towns and big cities turned to the soda shop for security and salvation when they couldn't drink. As one period writer explained, "Scientists tell us that gentlemen who formerly depended upon alcoholic beverages for general entertainment will now eat candy in large quantities and be for very strong soft drinks."[1]

Of course, gentlemen were not the only patrons of soda fountains and ice cream parlors. Different demographics demonstrated different preferences: "Men ask for fresh lime freezes, frozen mint juleps, orangeades and phosphates. Women are prone to order chocolate sundaes, fancy sundaes and the host of fancy, fluffy, creamy fountain specials. Old people usually take a dish of plain ice cream! The flappers like fancy sundaes especially fresh fruit frappes."[2]

Community streets changed as the dark, closed-up saloon walls made way for the bright, glass-windowed soda parlor. During 1920, the second year of prohibition in Ohio, which had "gone dry" in May 1919, the city of Cleveland reported "no less than 1,000 new [soda] fountains have been installed in almost as many new places." The sweeping changes happened all across the nation, as the "saloon no longer offers an attractive place in which [a] few minutes or hours may be whiled away, and the soda fountain has succeeded" in filling this role.[3]

All these customers kept the soda fountain man hopping. He was constantly "'Put to it' to devise variations of ice cream dishes for his patrons." These merchants, drugstore operators, and even former saloon owners found suggestions, recipes, business-building ideas, industry statistics, and a grand sense of ice-cream-delight boosterism in the pages of numerous trade journals.[4]

Thousands of specialty ice cream dishes were developed. Some of the fancifully named treats were described in those professional journals; others were never written down. A glance at a neighborhood soda fountain or ice cream parlor menu shows some of the variety of ice cream treats these men (yes, the owners were mostly male) created to feed a community hungry for both sweets and a place to hang out. In Stillwater, Minnesota, the menus from two neighboring soda parlors— Starkel's Pharmacy and St. Croix Drug Store—convey their stiff competition. With more than 150 items listed in "souvenir" menus, they touted their specialties and "fancy" sundaes and drinks to thirsty Stillwater folks. St. Croix Drug's eight-page menu, printed on a light beige stock, heralds the "Most Complete List of Delicious Ice Creams and Drinks in the City." Starkel's menu is cleverly tied with a colored ribbon and holds six pages that flip up to reveal 167 delightful and novel choices and claims of superiority: "If you know our Fountain Delicacies, then you know the best," and "The Ice Cream

used at our Fountain is made special for our use only." Patrons could order treats including Mexican, Chop Suey, or Boston Nut sundaes and "Ades" in flavors of lemon, lime, orange, or mint, along with a huge variety of sodas, frappés, or phosphates. If you didn't see what you wanted, just ask and the dispenser would "make it for you."[5]

With emerging Prohibition prospects, business opportunities quickly increased for entrepreneurial soda shop operators. The Eighteenth Amendment to the Constitution required only thirteen months to reach the required ratification by three-quarters of the states. The law took full effect on January 17, 1920, the capstone to efforts by the Women's Christian Temperance Society, the Anti-Saloon League, and other reform-minded organizations that had been working since the turn of the century to ban alcohol and drugs and "improve public morals."

During its sixteen-year history, Prohibition passed through the administrations of five presidents—Wilson, Harding, Coolidge, Hoover, and Franklin D. Roosevelt—however, one man's name is forever linked to the effort: Andrew J. Volstead, congressman from Minnesota. In 1919, it fell to Volstead, as head of the House Judiciary Committee, to write the legislation spelling out the specifics for enforcing the Eighteenth Amendment. Viewed nearly one hundred years later, Volstead seems to have been quiet and unassuming and complex. His wife had died the year before he was charged with writing the twelve-hundred-word regulation, and their only child, a daughter, now an adult, worked in his congressional office. He was not a temperance activist. He admitted to having enjoyed a drink of whiskey from time to time, when it was legal.

By 1921 Prohibition was in full swing, and the nation's soda fountain operators were taking advantage of the opportunities to serve law-abiding folks. In the pages of magazines and trade press, soda and sundae boosters offered tips, recipes, and a newsy view of the times. The recipes outlined top sellers, sundaes, specialty beverages, syrups, and dishes to serve in the "luncheonette," as many in the business realized a full-service menu was "what the people wanted, required, and demanded in the way of service . . . clean, well-prepared food with their soda fountain drinks."[6]

This was the era of soda fountains and speakeasies, racy automobiles, newfangled devices, fluctuating economic conditions, and—for those who dined, and drank, on the right side of the law—innovative beverages and exciting ice cream flavors, sundae varieties, and novelties, along with tasty luncheonette delights.

The pages that follow are a window into that world. Eavesdrop on suffragists and flappers, bootleggers and G-men, soda shop entrepreneurs, adventuring travelers, politicians, activists—both "wet" and "dry"—mothers, and some folks who told really corny jokes. Business tips and commentary on the times and the trade present a mirror of life and business in the soda fountain during the early days of Prohibition. Longer essays give some background into trends and events. And you'll find some delicious, easy-to-make recipes for treats that have disappeared but shouldn't have.

The recipes have been gathered from a number of publications written for soda fountain and ice cream parlor managers and operators. Together, they offer a typical representation of the time with one exception: recipes that included raw eggs as part of a soda or other dry beverage, though plentiful, have not been included.

ENJOYING THESE RECIPES

The recipes are straightforward. But you may want a few special items to make preparation and enjoyment easier.

MAKING ICE CREAM

No matter what device you use, these ice cream and sherbet recipes are relatively easy to make. I have three ice cream makers. My father's old hand-crank churn is at least thirty-five years old. It requires layering ice and salt outside the metal mixing canister with its wooden dasher. I have a newer—twenty-year-old—electric machine that still requires ice and salt. And then there is my newest, state-of-the-art electric machine. No ice. No salt. No fuss. I simply put the mixing canister in my freezer and pull it out when I want to make ice cream.

My ice cream makers reflect the wide variety available from gourmet stores and big-box discounters. Some still require the use of cracked ice and rock salt to freeze the mixture. These can be electrically powered or hand cranked. Other electric models use a core frozen for twenty-four hours which will then chill the ice cream mixture.

Three key things to remember:
First: Always follow the specific directions for your ice cream maker. These machines have different capacities. The one I've used to test these recipes is designed to make 1½ quarts of ice cream. I've found that putting in 3½ to 5 cups of mix works best. If your machine is smaller, you can churn the ice cream in batches. Just keep the mixture cold for up to three days in the refrigerator. If your machine is larger, you can always double these recipes for more delicious ice cream or sherbet.

Second: I've found the ice cream churns better and faster if you take the time to chill the mixture before you begin the actual ice cream–making process. Put the mixture in the refrigerator for several hours or in the freezer compartment for less time. Don't let it freeze beyond a thin layer around the edges: the churning does not go nearly as well if your ice cream mix is nearly frozen.

Third: When you finish churning, the ice cream will still be in a "soft serve" state. It needs to harden off, either sitting in the old-fashioned churn freshly packed with new layers of ice and salt or, for any kind of machine, spooned into an airtight container—the screw-top plastic ones work well—and placed in the freezer.

If you don't have an ice cream maker, you can still make these tasty treats. Put the mixture into a metal bowl and place it in the coldest part of your freezer. Take it out every couple of hours and beat the mixture with an electric mixer. It is helpful if you keep the beaters in the freezer, too.

SOME ADDITIONAL EQUIPMENT

Sundae and soda dishes and spoons: Tulip-shaped ice cream sundae glasses, long spoons, banana-split dishes, ice cream soda glasses with a ballooned-out top rim to hold in the soda bubbles—these can be found at a wide range of stores, from big-box discounters to gourmet kitchenware stores to antique shops. It is worth spending a few dollars to have a couple of these stylish glasses. Many of the sundaes are designed to be enjoyed as layers of flavor with an exuberant garnish at the very top. They just taste better when served in the flared glass. Long-handled spoons with a narrow bowl are perfect for getting the last bit of topping and ice cream from the bottom of the glass.

Ice cream scoops: Many period sundae and soda recipes specify the scoop size of ice cream by the size of the dipper. The original recipes may call for #20, #16, and #10 scoops, for example. The #20 dipper means twenty scoops from a quart, or about ⅓ cup. The #16 dipper means sixteen scoops from a quart, or ¼ cup. The #10 dipper means ten scoops from a quart, about ¾ cup. You can purchase ice cream scoopers by size in culinary departments and stores or online. For the recipes that follow, I'll just call them small, medium, and large. Of course, you can simply use a large spoon to approximate the amount.

Flavored syrups: Thanks to the trends for flavored coffees and home snow-cone machines, a wide variety of flavoring syrups are readily available in grocery stores, big-box stores, and coffee shops or from Internet sources. I've also included a recipe for "easy sampling syrups" in the Syrups and Fixings chapter (page 41).

One-half and one-ounce "jiggers": Useful for measuring out syrup servings, and easily found in the alcoholic beverage area of any store. There are simple substitutes. A standard ground-coffee measure is one ounce when filled "brim full," as are two tablespoons. However I think it is much easier—and oh so much more stylish—to dispense the syrups from the jigger, which is designed with extra room to prevent spillage.

Drink shaker: A wide-mouthed "cocktail" shaker with a strainer will give you the tool you need to easily mix and serve drinks made from milk, syrups, crushed ice, and ice cream. Or, if you don't happen to have one sitting about, you can use any approximately quart-sized container with a tight-fitting lid and a small

sieve to strain the liquid through. In the recipes that follow, I'll call it the "cocktail shaker," and you'll know what I mean.

Carbonated water: You can make your own carbonated or plain "sparkling" water and dispense it from a siphon device purchased from gourmet stores or on the Web. Or simply pick up carbonated water from the grocery store soda pop or water aisle. Do not use "tonic water," as it has a distinctive bitter taste. In the recipes I've suggested the amount of carbonated water you'll need for a tasty drink. For maximum fizz, don't measure: just pour it into the glass from your siphon or bottle of water. A typical twenty-ounce, "individual" bottle will be enough to make three of these Prohibition-era delights.

Ice cream toppings: There are recipes here for some of the more unusual toppings of the era, but most of the common ones from back then are readily available today.

Breweries and Main Streets
Find Salvation in Ice Cream

*"Kiewel Brewery will cease operation on June 30 as the law of the land . . .
in which the individual must submerge himself to the will of the masses . . .
We are encouraged in the belief that the same democratic operation
of governmental machinery will soon place at the disposal of the
American people light wines and beers."*

Public letter of appreciation from the Jacob Kiewel Brewing
Company, *Little Falls Daily Transcript*, July 1, 1919

THE NATION'S BREWERS, VINTNERS, and distillers had ample warning that Prohibition was coming and plenty of time to get their businesses in order. In August 1917, World War I food administrator Herbert Hoover ordered war-winning conservation restrictions on all distilled spirits made from any product that "could be used for food." Makers of whiskey and other high-proof beverages were to cease production. They could sell and transport what was already in their warehouses, but making new stocks was illegal. The rules were less strict for beer. As Hoover wrote to Senator Morris Sheppard of Texas, a noted temperance advocate—a "dry"—who was the original sponsor of the bill that would become the Eighteenth Amendment, there were benefits to allowing continued production of beer and wine.

Hoover explained, "If brewing were stopped today, beer would disappear from the liquor trade within one or two months and the whole country would be put practically on a whisky, brandy and gin basis with some supplies of wine. The saloons would be left open upon a basis of selling drinks carrying 40 per cent or 50 per cent alcohol, with some small supplies of wine, instead of a large proportion of their customers being served with a drink of 2¾ per cent alcoholic content and therefore, from a temperance viewpoint, much less harmful."[1]

The arrival of World War I was a timely boost for temperance activists. Now, after fifty years of work and some successes in more rural states, the Anti-Saloon League and others could bootstrap national prohibition onto war concerns. The time was right, the temperance activists knew, to free the nation from alcoholic temptations and, as the name of the leading prohibition organization indicated, to

7

remove the saloon, the evil purveyor of those temptations, from every Main Street corner. The success of the Anti-Saloon League was astounding. The Eighteenth Amendment, ordering national prohibition, passed through Congress and was ratified by the states faster than almost anyone thought possible. The legislation allowed seven years to accomplish ratification by thirty-six states. It took just one.

Although the Eighteenth Amendment specified a year from ratification until enforcement, the War Prohibition Act, passed by Congress just a few days before the armistice, still came into full effect on July 1, 1919, seven months after peace was declared. An economic and food conservation case for going ahead with those war restrictions was argued. President Wilson, for example, had pledged huge quantities of grain and other foods to continue helping European Allies and even to begin rebuilding war-torn Germany. Yet Wilson urged Congress to repeal the wartime restrictions, saying the objectives had been met. Instead, Congress combined enforcement measures with legislation, leaving Wilson no choice but to veto the Volstead enforcement act. Wilson feared that lumping the wartime restrictions in with those of the Eighteenth Amendment might make the law unconstitutional. In his veto statement the president declared: "In all matters having to do with the personal habits and customs of large numbers of our people we must be certain that the established processes of legal change are followed." Congress overrode his veto in record time. From a practical point of view, the combined act now required brewers to join distillers.

No more alcoholic beverages could be made after July 1, 1919.[2]

When these laws took effect the number of alcohol-related businesses was significant. The nation had 507 distilleries with an annual output of 288 million gallons of distilled spirits of various kinds. There were 1,217 breweries with an output of hundreds of millions of gallons of beer. More than five hundred warehouses contained practically 200 million gallons of intoxicating liquor, and, last but not least, there were 178,000 saloons nationwide.[3]

Through the first months of Prohibition enforcement, many brewers, vintners, and labor leaders remained hopeful that Congress would come to its senses, temper the strict Prohibition restrictions, and restore the agreeable war limits so that at least 2¾ percent beer and light wines could be sold. But the Prohibitionists and the government stuck to the one-half percent alcohol limit, and the brewers were saddled with large buildings in need of alternative uses. The decisions and actions of the Kiewel Brewery in Little Falls, Minnesota, demonstrates how aggressive business practices enabled this family-owned company to survive and positioned it well for whatever opportunities might come. For Kiewel and many more breweries around the country, ice cream equaled salvation.

The three-story yellow brick Kiewel Brewery stood on the corner of Seventh Street and Fifth Avenue Northwest in Little Falls. It covered half a block with a footprint of more than twelve thousand square feet. Jacob Kiewel and four of his sons incorporated in 1906. They remodeled the original frame structure, building a modern brewery. Under Prohibition, in

1920 they remodeled again, shifting their business from a yearly production of fifteen thousand barrels of 4 percent White Rose lager beer—brewed from Minnesota hops and malt, providing "health-giving, tissue-building and nerve-strengthening qualities"—to nonalcoholic malt beverages, near beer, butter, condensed milk, and ice cream.[4]

The *Little Falls Daily Transcript* reported the events. As the Kiewel plant remodeling advanced, the north half of the building continued to make nonalcoholic malt beverages. Soon the three stories of the south half were completely restructured. The walls were painted a sanitary white. The finest equipment of the day was installed. The first floor of the old malt house became the receiving room for the daily production of fifteen thousand cows. From there the milk and cream were pumped to the second-floor creamery. Inside the ice cream room, white, vitrified ice cream freezers with silver tops churned away, making the standard vanilla and chocolate as well as "Palmer House" and other specialty flavors. The finished ice cream was stored in four cork-insulated cooler rooms. The reporter ended the article optimistically, quoting management that "If the occasion presents itself, the Kiewel company can make beer on short notice."[5]

Thirteen years later the plant did swing back into the brewing business. After eleven weeks of remodeling, a crew of more than twenty men started making beer in the fall of 1933. Although Kiewel management stated they would continue to operate the ice cream and creamery products line alongside the forty-thousand-barrel brewery, nine months later the demand for beer was so strong that production expanded back into the full plant.[6]

In the intervening years, though, reports across the country noted the flourishing ice cream culture in the wake of Prohibition-closed saloons and breweries. *The Expositor,* a national magazine with a religious content and audience, highlighted the experience of "one Eastern city," until recently home to three breweries. That city had been drinking about 300,000 barrels of beer yearly, which sold at retail for about $4.2 million: "Today the city is eating 3,000,000 gallons of ice cream. It formerly drank about a barrel per capita each year[;] now its annual consumption of ice cream is about eight gallons per year." In New Orleans, according to the *International Confectioner,* "Anheuser-Busch was watching their beer drinkers frothing at the mouth and making onslaughts upon the ice cream parlors and that set them to thinking. They had a fine beer bottling branch house in New Orleans and they are now turning it into an ice cream factory."[7]

Current Opinion magazine published a comprehensive story on the state of one of the nation's leading brewing cities: St. Louis, it reported, "never has been so prosperous, so busy, so ambitious or so confident as today." The article detailed thirty-three breweries, employing fifteen thousand persons, that had been shut down along with 2,500 saloons. But more than seven hundred new grocery stores had opened, and there were few vacant business properties and practically no vacant residences: "There is no unemployment, the hotels have no vacant rooms, the boarding houses are filled."[8]

As to the workers and the brewery physical plants, there was good news for them, too. The new General Motors plant absorbed the fifteen thousand former employees of the breweries and allied trades, and the new Union Drug Company plant was ready to take as many more. The great Anheuser-Busch plant was refitted: part of it into packing plants, part into a sausage factory, part into a manufactory of a new soft drink. The Union Brewery was transformed into an oleomargarine factory, while the Mutual Brewery became an automobile assembling plant and the Home Brewery simply became a cold storage plant. The Griesedieck Brewery shifted to manufacturing commercial alcohol, which was needed for industrial purposes and highly regulated. And finally, the Schorr-Kolkschneider Brewery made ice cream.[9]

THE ORGANIZATION that had propelled temperance activism into successful passage of the Eighteenth Amendment was the Anti-Saloon League. Founded in 1893 in Oberlin, Ohio, the group gained strength two years later when it merged with a similar organization based in the nation's capital. Acting with forceful dedication to their motto—"The saloon must go"—the Anti-Saloon League realized that if it could influence and motivate just 10 percent of the electorate, those votes would be enough to change national policy. The group communicated through church-based peer group outreach and a flood of support materials. At its height in the 1910s, the league printed and disseminated forty tons of reading material—books, flyers, newspapers, and brochures—a month.[10]

Wayne Wheeler was tapped to join the league leadership in its first year, when he was a twenty-three-year-old student at Oberlin College. He dedicated his life to the goal of an alcohol-free nation. Wheeler attended law school because the organization needed a lawyer, and he became a feared advocate, or adversary, in the halls of Congress. Once Prohibition passed, he prosecuted more than two thousand dry law cases. His disdain for alcohol can be traced to a serious injury he received in childhood from a drunken pitchfork-wielding neighbor.[11]

The Anti-Saloon League literature played heavily on the sympathetic plight of mothers and children whose fathers spent their time and money in the corner saloon. The black-ink line drawing on one emotionally charged flyer showed a mother and her son under the headline "Daddy's in There," with the caption "And our Shoes and Stockings and Clothes and Food Are in There, Too, and They'll Never Come Out."

The message concluded with a poem:

A Father Wanted
Julia H. Johnson

It was there that he saw his father
But the man only shook his head
And the boy, with his thin cheek burning,
Ran away with a look of dread.

Oh the fathers—the fathers wanted!
How the heart-break, and bitter need,
With the longings, deep and piteous,
For the wandering children plead.

May the children's call around them,
May the fathers arise and go
With the young souls waiting for them
For the little ones need them so![12]

There were saloons, plenty of them, on the nation's corners. Most of them were owned, controlled, or bankrolled by the major beer producers as an important part of their business structure. So now in addition to finding alternative purposes to keep the breweries active, their owners needed to deal with soon-to-be-shuttered corner saloons. The Joseph Schlitz Brewing Company of Milwaukee owned four hundred choice saloon rooms in that city and more than fifteen hundred buildings throughout the country.[13]

The early experience in Grand Rapids, Michigan, which enacted statewide prohibition ahead of the national law, provides an indication of the outcome. One third of the saloons became ice cream and soda fountain parlors, another third hoped for return to alcohol and bided their time serving soft drinks, and the final third, located on less desirable corners, closed. The *Anti-Saloon League Yearbook* for 1920 suggests the corner saloons had "simply been converted into other places of business producing and selling in most cases that which ministers to the comfort and prosperity of the people of the country."[14]

However, in the case of one brewer, liquidating these real estate investments made a significant impact. As August Busch recounted, "We used to own the corner saloon . . . The gas stations paid us a fortune for them because we had the best locations. That was the thing that saved Anheuser-Busch."[15]

Salvation for the brewers and for Main Street aside, an exchange between an anonymous brewery owner and an equally unknown commentator quoted in the *Expositor* brought the purpose of the deeper dedication to Prohibition into focus: "A certain Ohio brewery recently converted into a malted-milk plant, now employs 217 men where formerly only 78 were engaged. The business has been changed and the plant enlarged at very little expense. Someone remarked to the head of the concern who was expressing his satisfaction at the change in his business. 'You feed babies now instead of starving them.'

"'I guess you are right,'" was the reply.[16]

FUTURIST SUNDAE

1 small scoop vanilla ice cream

1 small scoop chocolate ice cream

2 tablespoons chocolate syrup

2 tablespoons crushed pineapple

whipped cream for topping

crystallized ginger

maraschino cherry

mint sprigs for garnish

Put the ice cream in a banana split dish. Pour chocolate syrup over the vanilla ice cream and pineapple over the chocolate ice cream. Top with whipped cream, and place strips of crystallized ginger on the vanilla side. Put the cherry in between the ice creams, and garnish with fresh mint.

ICE CREAMS AND SHERBETS

Since the advent of prohibition, ice cream has become more popular than ever before. Chocolate, vanilla, and strawberry are the flavors most in demand . . . The names attached to a sundae which is usually a ball of ice cream surrounded with syrup, whipped cream, nuts, cherries or what not, are sometimes misleading and often strange: 'Broadway,' 'Merry Widow,' 'Orphan's Delight,' 'Banana Royal,' and 'Chop Suey' are some of the sundae names.

"ICE CREAM HABIT GROWN," *NEW YORK TIMES*, AUGUST 14, 1927

THE TEMPERANCE PERSPECTIVE

"And this sober world is on the horizon . . . The world as a whole had finally and definitely wearied of a half-crazed humanity. It is tired of a misnomer civilization with a saloon on every other street corner filled with sodden victims, dead to everything but desire and selfish gratification. There are long and dangerous bridges to be crossed, but no analytical student of the situation had the remotest doubt about the ultimate result." —Randolph Wellford Smith, *The Sober World*

Plain Vanilla Ice Cream

4 cups rich cream (or a mixture of half-and-half, milk, or heavy cream), divided

1 cup sugar

3 teaspoons vanilla extract

In a small saucepan, combine 2 cups of the cream, or milk and cream mixture, and the sugar. Cook over low heat, stirring until the sugar is dissolved. Remove from the heat and add the remaining cream and vanilla. Chill the mixture and then freeze following the directions of your ice cream maker.

NOTE: See tips for making ice cream starting on page 4.

The American workers demand and
are entitled to ice cream and automobiles.

SAMUEL GOMPERS, QUOTED IN *THE SODA FOUNTAIN*, SEPTEMBER 1921

SODA SHOPS TO TAKE ADVANTAGE OF PROHIBITION

"Don't forget that national prohibition will be with us June 30th and is bound to make an undreamed volume of business—for those who are ready. Are you ready? We are ready and want you to know it . . . we have made only the best quality fountains and everything which goes with them. They are the best and most for the money." —Liquid Carbonic Company advertisement, *The International Confectioner,* January 1919

Frozen Custard

1 cup sugar

2 teaspoons cornstarch

4 cups milk

2 eggs

3 teaspoons vanilla extract

In a medium saucepan, combine the sugar and cornstarch. Gradually add the milk. Cook over low heat, stirring frequently until the sugar is dissolved and the mixture is thickened. In a small heatproof container, beat the eggs. Then, very gradually and stirring constantly, add some of the hot milk mixture to the eggs so that they are tempered—that is, raised to the temperature of the simmering milk. Add this mixture back to the saucepan and continue to cook over low heat, stirring constantly, until completely thickened, about 5 minutes. Cool, stir in the vanilla, and chill the mixture before freezing following the directions of your ice cream maker.

SODA FOUNTAIN OWNERS, "EDUCATE YOUR CUSTOMERS"

"The soda fountain and the delicious beverages and ice cream served over its shining marble surface will play a greater part in the every day lives of the American public than ever before. In the next few months our entire country will be on a prohibition basis, and while the national thirst will remain the same, the national supply of thirst quenchers will be of the soft variety. Every soda fountain owner must bestir himself now . . . The established soda fountain should secure a big share of the new trade, but it will not get any unless efforts are made to interest new customers and educate them on the qualities of ice cream and soft drinks."
—The International Confectioner, February 1919

Orange Ice Cream

¾ cup unsweetened frozen orange juice concentrate, thawed (see note, below)
1¼ cups water
1⅛ cups sugar
½ cup milk
⅓ cup heavy cream

Combine the orange juice concentrate with water in a medium saucepan, add the sugar, and heat gradually until the sugar is dissolved, stirring from time to time. Remove from heat. Add the milk and cream, mixing well. Chill the mixture and then freeze following the directions of your ice cream maker.

NOTE: A 12-ounce container of frozen orange juice concentrate is enough for two batches of ice cream.

Coffee Ice Cream

This delightful ice cream is lightly crystalline
with a refreshing melt-in-your-mouth flavor.

⅓ cup sugar

1 cup hot, strong black coffee

2 cups milk

1 cup heavy cream

Dissolve the sugar in the coffee. Add the milk and cream. Chill the mixture and
then freeze following the directions of your ice cream maker.

Feed the children ice cream and give them a
pint of milk each day. You will see that it improves
their entire mental machinery.

DR. E. W. FAHEY, DIRECTOR OF PUBLIC HEALTH, DULUTH, MINNESOTA, 1921

HOW PROHIBITION PASSED THROUGH STATE LEGISLATURES

"I was at a dinner about ten days ago at which some seven members of the legislature were present, all of whom had voted to ratify the prohibition amendment . . . I asked one of them why he voted for prohibition, and he told me this—it may have been an excuse; may have been a reason—he said, 'When this question came up everybody interested in prohibition in my district wrote me a letter. Every church organization that was interested wrote me letters; they sent people to see me; they sent delegations and urged me to vote for prohibition. No one approached me to urge me not to vote for prohibition except for two members from my district, both of whom were saloonkeepers and men of no particular standing.' 'Well,' I said, 'did you ever count up the anti-prohibition vote in your own district?' He said, 'We never had any to count!' Well now that is just the situation. That is the way prohibition was passed.

"I think without doubt you are facing the biggest ice cream year that you have ever known. I don't know how much money you are going to make, but you are going to sell more ice cream than you ever did in your lives—no question about that." —Walter J. Carlin, Council for National Confectioners Association, "Ice Cream Troubles," *The International Confectioner,* April 1919

Maple Mousse Ice Cream

The delicate maple flavor is enhanced by a bit of bittersweet chocolate topping. It has a rich mouthfeel and makes a delicious ice cream cone.

1 envelope unflavored gelatin (Knox brand)
2 tablespoons cold water
1 cup milk
⅔ cup sugar
2 teaspoons freshly squeezed lemon juice
2 cups heavy cream
⅔ cup real maple syrup
2 teaspoons vanilla extract

In a small bowl, sprinkle the gelatin over the cold water, stir, and let stand to soften. In a medium saucepan, combine the milk and the sugar. Cook over low heat, stirring occasionally until the sugar is dissolved. Remove from the heat and add the gelatin mixture, stirring until it is fully dissolved. Add the lemon juice, stirring rapidly so that the juice mixes immediately and does not form soured clumps. Add the cream, maple syrup, and vanilla, mixing well. Chill the mixture and then freeze following the directions of your ice cream maker.

TAKE SOME ICE CREAM HOME

"There are, however, thousands of families who never think of serving [ice cream] on their tables as they do not realize it is possible to carry home a well wrapped brick of ice cream and serve it in good shape an hour later. Many of these people would gladly be our ice cream patrons if they realized how easily it could be obtained." —F. H. Bothell, "Place of Ice Cream in Dairy Industry," *The International Confectioner,* April 1919

Bisque Ice Cream

½ cup sugar

1 teaspoon cornstarch

2 cups milk

1 egg

1½ teaspoons vanilla extract

12 macaroons

1½ cups sherry wine

2 cups heavy cream

4 ounces (about 1 cup) slivered almonds, toasted and finely chopped

In a medium saucepan, combine the sugar and cornstarch. Gradually add the milk. Cook over low heat, stirring from time to time until the sugar is dissolved and the mixture is thickened. In a small heatproof container such as a glass measuring cup or coffee mug, beat the egg. Then, very gradually, add some of the hot milk mixture, stirring constantly, so that the egg is tempered and raised to the temperature of the milk. Add this mixture back to the remaining milk and continue to cook until completely thickened, about 5 minutes over very low heat. Remove from heat, add vanilla, and put this base into the refrigerator to chill. While the base is chilling, crumble the macaroons into the wine and set aside.

When you are ready to freeze the ice cream: beat the heavy cream until it forms soft peaks. Drain and discard any unabsorbed wine from the macaroons. Fold the macaroons and almonds into the base and then fold mixture into the whipped cream. Freeze following the directions of your ice cream maker.

AN ODE TO A BAR-ROOM

Hush little bar-room,
Don't you cry,
You'll be a fountain
Bye and Bye!

D. O. HAYNES AND COMPANY, PUBLISHERS,
THE INTERNATIONAL CONFECTIONER, APRIL 1919

BREWERIES BEGIN CHURNING ICE CREAM

"From every State news comes that breweries are being changed into other lines. A list of breweries going into soft drinks is already above the 100 mark and fully 30 are going into ice cream. Many are going into the milk business . . . Cold storage, laundry, syrups, ice, dry storage are some of the lines being taken up. In the south it is soft drinks and near beer." —The International Confectioner, May 1919

Bostonian Nut Ice Cream

This rich, luscious ice cream is smooth and oh, so tasty! It has quickly become a family favorite.

3 eggs, well beaten
2 cups firmly packed brown sugar
1⅓ cups heavy cream
2⅔ cups half-and-half
2⅔ teaspoons vanilla extract
2¾ ounces (⅔ cup) finely chopped pecans

In a medium saucepan with a heavy bottom, combine the eggs, sugar, cream, and half-and-half. Stir over low heat until the sugar is dissolved, then continue cooking over very low heat or in a double boiler over simmering water, stirring constantly to prevent lumps and scorching (see note, page 23), until the mixture is thick enough to coat the back of a spoon and when you run your finger through it there is a clear line. This could take 15 minutes or longer. Once the mixture is thickened, remove from heat and cool. Stir in the vanilla and chill the mixture before putting it into your ice cream maker. Add the nuts when the ice cream is nearly churned. (If you can't make additions while the machine is working, add the nuts at the beginning.)

NOTE: If by chance you do end up with some lumps in the ice cream base, all is not lost. Simply press the mixture through a fine sieve to remove them and then continue with the chilling and freezing.

Caramel Ice Cream

Not as sweet as the Bostonian Nut, but with a similar flavor profile, this ice cream brings a sophisticated end to the perfect dinner. Lovely as is, it's even better topped with bittersweet Hot Chocolate Fudge Sundae Sauce (page 42).

1½ cups milk
1 egg
⅓ cup firmly packed brown sugar
¼ cup caramel syrup
¼ teaspoon salt
1½ teaspoons vanilla extract
1½ cups heavy cream

Heat the milk in a heavy 2-quart saucepan or double boiler just until it begins to bubble around the edges. In a small bowl, lightly beat the egg and stir in the sugar. Add some of the hot milk very gradually to warm the egg mixture. Then stir this heated egg, sugar, and milk mixture back into the scalded milk and cook over low heat, stirring constantly, until the mixture is thickened. Cool to room temperature; stir in the caramel syrup, salt, and vanilla. Chill this custard base mixture in the refrigerator. Whip the heavy cream until it forms soft peaks. Gently fold the custard base into the whipped cream and then freeze following the directions of your ice cream maker.

RECIPE NOTE: MAKING SHERBET WITH EGG WHITES

Many of the original 1920s sherbet recipes on the following pages included raw egg whites, which were whipped and folded into the sherbet mix when it was nearly frozen. I prefer not to prepare recipes with raw egg whites, so I've substituted pasteurized meringue powder, which can be found in the grocery store baking aisle. It doesn't whip up as well as a raw egg white would, but it still works to stabilize and lighten the mixture. Mix the powder with cold water and lightly whip, then add to the sherbet mixture and freeze.

Canton Ginger Sherbet

A crisp, refreshing icy sherbet.

¼ pound fresh ginger, peeled and thinly sliced
1 cup sugar
3½ cups water
½ cup freshly squeezed orange juice
¼ cup freshly squeezed lemon juice
1 tablespoon dry meringue powder
2 tablespoons cold water

In a medium saucepan, combine the ginger, sugar, and 3½ cups water. Simmer for 15 minutes. Remove from the heat and cool slightly. Strain to remove the ginger. Add the fruit juices and chill. When ready to freeze the sherbet, sprinkle the meringue powder over the 2 tablespoons cold water. Stir to blend and then whip until the mixture begins to form soft peaks. It will not whip as high as a regular egg white. Fold the whipped meringue mixture into the ginger sherbet mix and freeze following the directions of your ice cream maker.

Cranberry and Raisin Sherbet

1 (12- to 14-ounce) package cranberries (see note, below)
1 cup raisins, coarsely chopped
1¼ cups water
1½ cups sugar
1 tablespoon meringue powder
2 tablespoons cold water

In a medium saucepan, combine the cranberries, raisins, and 1¼ cups water. Cook over medium heat until the berries pop and then become very tender, about 10 minutes. Cool slightly. Run the mixture through a food mill or press through a coarse sieve with a wooden spoon. Discard the cranberry skin remnants. Return the cranberry and raisin puree to the saucepan and add the sugar. Cook over medium heat, stirring occasionally, until the sugar is dissolved. Chill the mixture.

When ready to freeze the sherbet, sprinkle the meringue powder over the 2 tablespoons cold water. Stir to blend and then whip until the mixture begins to form soft peaks. It will not whip as high as a regular egg white. Fold the whipped meringue mixture into the sherbet mix and freeze following the directions of your ice cream maker.

NOTE: If cranberries are frozen, no need to thaw: simply put the frozen berries into the water.

> There was a boy named Herbert,
> Who tried some of our sherbet—
> He ate all we had
> And said he, "Egad,
> You'll get rich, you deserve it."
>
> *THE SODA FOUNTAIN, AUGUST 1922*

DRIPPING-WET JOKES WRUNG OUT OF THE THEATERS

"Patrons of the [vaudeville] playhouse, it is understood, have complained so persistently of the great number of vaudevillians who ring in a joke, or a gibe, or a sentimental wheeze based on the dry law and its enforcement that the management decided it was to the best interests of every one concerned that a strict regulation be made." —Mixer and Server, September 15, 1922

Pineapple Frost

"This is an unusually delicious dish and can be sold for fifteen cents."

1 envelope unflavored gelatin (Knox brand)

2 tablespoons cold water

1 (14- to 16-ounce) can crushed pineapple
   packed in juice, drained, juice reserved

2 cups water, approximately

1½ cups sugar

freshly squeezed juice of 1 lemon

freshly squeezed juice of ½ orange

In a small bowl, sprinkle the gelatin over the 2 tablespoons of cold water, stir, and set aside. Combine the reserved pineapple juice with enough water to make 2½ cups. In a medium saucepan, combine the juice and water mixture and sugar. Simmer, over low heat, stirring from time to time, until the sugar is completely dissolved. Remove from heat. Add the softened gelatin and mix until it is completely dissolved, then add the crushed pineapple and lemon and orange juices. If necessary, put the mixture in a blender and pulse until the pineapple pieces are no larger than half of a pencil eraser. Put the mixture in the refrigerator to chill and then freeze following the directions of your ice cream machine.

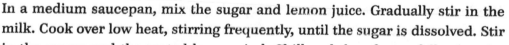

Lemon Cream Sherbet

Just tart enough to be a refreshing family favorite.

1 cup sugar

¼ cup freshly squeezed lemon juice

1 cup milk

1⅔ cups half-and-half

grated rind of one small lemon (about 1 loosely packed tablespoon)

In a medium saucepan, mix the sugar and lemon juice. Gradually stir in the milk. Cook over low heat, stirring frequently, until the sugar is dissolved. Stir in the cream and the grated lemon rind. Chill and then freeze following the directions of your ice cream maker.

Young wife: "Do you know anything that will remove wine-stains from the tablecloth?"
Her catty aunt: "Yes, Prohibition!"

THE SPATULA JANUARY 1921

THE FOOD VALUE OF ICE CREAM

"Bread, butter and ice cream, however, constitute a very acceptable mid-day luncheon or supper . . . Fruit sauces are eaten very largely for the flavor they impart to the bread, which lacks flavor. Ice cream may be used in the place of fruit preserves and is superior in bringing much more protein and energy than the fruits and in furnishing vitamins which the fruit lacks altogether . . . I would put in more such ice cream parlors in conjunction with fruit stands and let them gradually take the place of the American saloon." —Professor R. M. Washburn, "Fat Standards and Food Values in Ice Cream," *The International Confectioner,* January 1919

Grape Ice Cream

This beautiful, light lavender ice cream packs perfectly into an ice cream cone and is a favorite of sophisticated tasters who long for youthful flavors.

1 envelope unflavored gelatin (Knox brand)
3 tablespoons cold water
1½ cups whole milk
1 cup sugar
1¼ cups heavy cream
½ cup frozen grape juice concentrate, thawed

In a small dish, sprinkle the gelatin over the cold water and set aside. In a small saucepan, heat milk just until it begins to bubble around the edges and then add the sugar, stirring until it is dissolved. Remove pan from the heat. Stir in the gelatin mixture, making sure it is completely dissolved. Let cool. Stir in the heavy cream and then the grape juice concentrate. Chill and then freeze following the directions of your ice cream maker.

NOTE: Because of the gelatin, the mixture will set up like a Bavarian cream before you freeze it. This makes for a delightful finished ice cream texture.

GRAPE'S UNEXPECTED PROHIBITION POPULARITY

The flavor of the grape always has been in great demand. With the passage of the Volstead Act it was feared by the grape growers that grapes would not find a ready market for the volume use that had been in alcoholic beverages. To their great surprise, it was found that people still like grape, unfermented, as well as fermented.

CANDY AND SODA PROFITS, APRIL 1921

Ice Cream Bombe

1 pint strawberry ice cream
1 pint pineapple sherbet
crushed fresh or frozen strawberries for serving

Chill a metal decorative mold or mixing bowl. Spoon the strawberry ice cream into the mold and press evenly up against the sides. Fill the center with pineapple sherbet. Press a piece of plastic wrap across the surface of the sherbet and cover with foil. Return to the freezer to set up for at least 2 hours. To serve, slice and top with crushed strawberries.

Apricot Ice Cream

1 (8-ounce) can apricots packed in juice
1½ pints good-quality vanilla ice cream such as Plain Vanilla (page 14)
    or Ben and Jerry's

Process or blend the apricots and juice until finely chunked but not yet a smooth puree. Place in a 2-quart bowl and refrigerate to chill both the apricots and the bowl. Soften the ice cream in the refrigerator. Blend the two mixtures. Repack in sturdy containers with lids that close tightly and refreeze.

Tutti Frutti Ice Cream

1 quart good-quality vanilla ice cream such as Plain Vanilla (page 14)
  or Ben and Jerry's

2 cups mixed fruits such as candied cherries, raisins soaked in ½ cup
  brandy and patted dry, or candied citron (found in the "fruitcake
  ingredients" section during the holidays)

Soften ice cream slightly in the microwave or refrigerator. Stir in the fruit and
refreeze in a plastic container. Stir once or twice during the refreezing process
to help distribute the fruits evenly.

A TASTY NEW ICE CREAM

A new combination is peanut butter and
seedless raisins. This costs less than tutti fruitti
and will become as popular if the peanut butter
is fresh and not too much is used in a batch.

THE INTERNATIONAL CONFECTIONER, JUNE 1919

CONFIDENCE IN PROHIBITION SUCCESS

"I am proud that America is leading in this great movement. The eyes of the world are upon us, and from innumerable homes, here and beyond the seas, prayers go up for the success of the cause. Are we going to disappoint them? No! A thousand times no! The men and women who wrote the prohibition amendment into the National Constitution will, I am sure, sustain it. A nation that was brave enough and generous enough to give millions of its men and billions of its money in the World War will turn aside with contempt from the sneers and taunts of those who selfishly and petulantly insist that their right to indulge in intoxicating drinks is superior to all law and more important than the public good." —Congressman Andrew Volstead

George Washington Ice Cream

The original recipe used just water and juice for a granular "ice." Our family likes this ice cream version, adapted from other period sources but keeping the cherry flavors.

1⅓ teaspoons unflavored gelatin
    (Knox brand)

¼ cup cold water

1 (10-ounce) jar maraschino cherries

1⅓ cups milk, approximately

1¾ cups sugar

½ cup cherry juice, bottled or frozen

1¼ cups half-and-half

Sprinkle the gelatin over the cold water, stir, and let stand until softened. Drain the cherries, putting the juice into a 2-cup glass measuring cup. Coarsely chop the cherries and set aside. Add milk to the maraschino cherry juice to make 2 cups. Place juice, milk, and sugar in a medium saucepan and cook over low heat, stirring until the sugar has dissolved. Remove from heat and stir in the softened gelatin. Add remaining cherry juice and half-and-half, and then stir in the chopped cherries. Chill the mixture and then freeze following the directions of your ice cream maker.

AFTERNOON DATE IN A SODA FOUNTAIN

I went to a fountain with Mary
And met with an awful mishap;
For I awkwardly emptied a glassful
Of grape-juice all over her lap.
But Mary was gentle and gracious
(for none is so tactful as she),
And, smiling with perfect composure,
Said sweetly, "The drinks are on me."

PRACTICAL DRUGGIST AND PHARMACEUTICAL REVIEW OF REVIEWS, 1921

The Price Paid by Andrew Volstead

"Having sponsored this law and the enforcement cause in the House, much bitterness and abuse has been directed against me personally and as a consequence my name has in a measure become synonymous with the prohibition policy. No one here can doubt my attitude on the prohibition question. You are all aware of the work I have done in trying to place upon the statute books an effective enforcement law."

"Volstead Claims Credit," *New York Times*, February 24, 1922

NINE-TERM MINNESOTA CONGRESSMAN Andrew Volstead was just doing his job. As newly selected chairman of the House Judiciary Committee, he was responsible for writing the law providing the specific enforcement structure, rules, and penalties for the Eighteenth Amendment—a statement of policy that was a bit longer than one hundred words. Interviewing him in November 1921, nearly a year after the law named after him went into effect, James Morrow of the *St. Louis Post Dispatch* described the congressman's motivation, reporting that Volstead was not a devoted temperance activist: "He wrote the bill that bears his name solely because the law must have a strong arm."

Although Volstead relied upon the research and ideas of Wayne Wheeler, legislative lawyer for the Anti-Saloon League, a major activist group responsible for enactment of Prohibition, in the end it was Volstead who wrote the legislation and then marshaled it through

Congress. And it was Volstead who, rather quickly, paid the political and personal price with reelection difficulties, scorn from fellow members of Congress, hate mail, and even death threats. Among the letters in the Volstead manuscript collection at the Minnesota Historical Society are newspaper clippings that had been illustrated with photographs of the congressman. Letter writers mounted those pictures on cardboard so they could tie a kitchen-string noose around "Volsdead's" neck before sending them to Washington.

Once the Eighteenth Amendment was ratified by the states—and rather more quickly than anyone expected—the stage was set for the next step, contentious passage of the enforcement legislation. While the Senate passed the bill easily by a voice vote, the tally was far from unanimous in the House, where the "Volstead Act" passed 287 to 100. Two weeks later, legislators were shocked when President Woodrow Wilson vetoed the bill on October 27, 1919, citing its inclusion of the wartime prohibition restrictions along with the new national ban. Both houses quickly voted to override Wilson's veto. With some political maneuvering orchestrated by the leadership and Volstead, the House acted at light speed, "ramming" through the vote in the early evening the day Wilson's veto was delivered—and while at least fifty "wet"-voting congressmen were absent. It passed 176 to 55. The Senate passed it the following day.[1]

During the initial deliberations, Volstead had characterized the enforcement act as sensible: "The aim of the committee has been to present a measure that would, if enacted into law, carry into effect in good faith the purpose of this amendment, and would not present any feature to which any law-abiding citizen could reasonably object." However, not everyone agreed, including some of Andrew Volstead's constituents back in southwestern Minnesota. He was nearly voted out of office before the law could take effect in January 1921.[2]

In the summer of 1920, Volstead lost his party's primary to Rev. O. J. Kvale. Volstead supporters brought suit, charging the minister with violations of the Minnesota corrupt practices act. The case claimed that campaign materials printed and circulated by Kvale had said Volstead was an atheist and opposed to the Bible and further alleged that he had sneeringly made allusions to Kvale's preaching on the miracle of the loaves and fishes. In finding for Volstead, the judge asserted that Kvale's acts "constitute a deliberate, serious and material violation of the laws of the state . . . and that there is no jus-

tification or excuse therefore." He also awarded the nomination to Volstead.[3]

Kvale appealed the decision to the Minnesota Supreme Court and, while he didn't win, neither did Volstead. The court modified the lower court's decision, eliminating the clause declaring Volstead the nominee. Then the state Republican Party selected Volstead as the nominee, and he went on to win reelection in 1920.[4]

Two years later, in the election of 1922, the stakes were even higher. Volstead explained on the House floor that "the wet organizations are at work today in my district and have been for months. They have made all sorts of threats of what they are going to do to me. I have had to face all sorts of abuse and I expect to face a great deal more of it. I am willing to meet all fair criticism, but when a person falsely impugns my motives I resent it as vigorously as I can."[5]

Once again Rev. Kvale was Congressman Volstead's opponent. This time, however, Kvale had switched parties and defeated Volstead in the general election. Three years after the Volstead Act went into effect, Andrew Volstead returned to Granite Falls to practice law.

In between those two elections, St. Louis reporter Morrow interviewed Congressman Volstead. He depicted a tall, "thin, bushy-haired, heavy-mustached and grey-eyed citizen of Granite Falls, Minnesota." Morrow also described some of the correspondence that had arrived in Volstead's office during the nearly two years the Volstead Act had been in effect: "Letters that he has received and is receiving unsigned largely show vigorously enough and even profanely, that the wrath of the alcoholic hosts of the republic center upon him." In addition to the string-noose threats, hundreds of writers castigated Volstead's prohibition actions for a variety of reasons ranging from personal to patriotic.

In June 1921, Ed. McHoltz, a "100% American" from Zanesville, Ohio, wrote under the heading "Free America? (for some)": "If it were not for a bunch of nuts like you and a few more, we would be enjoying a nice cool glass of beer these hot days."[6]

A gentleman from Diggins, Missouri, who would have been twenty during the Civil War, put a historically positive spin on the enjoyment of alcoholic beverages: "I am 80 years old. You and your coterie will never be able to enforce the Volstead act and if you think you can you are doomed to disappointment and defeat. George Washington, Thomas Jefferson, Henry Clay, Daniel Webster, U. S. Grant[,] W. T. Sherman, Andrew Johnson, Andrew Jackson and thousands of others drank real liquor, brandy and wine and the most of them kept a good supply all the time. All these noble men were as good morally and most of them better than you are and all of them were men of much greater ability than you and any of your coterie. Respectfully W. P. Doran."[7]

Not all the correspondence was negative or hate filled. Scores of letters of support came from temperance groups, individuals, and even businesses. An unsigned and undated letter praised Volstead's accomplishments: "You are certainly entitled to great credit for what you have done to make our nation more nearly a Sober Nation." John A. O'Connor of Bal-

timore described the beneficial effects of Prohibition in his neighborhood just sixteen months after the law took effect: "It's amazing to meet individuals whom I knew a year ago as loafers, down-and-outers, tramps, pan handlers and sots in my work of reform transformed into sober and industrious men and women through prohibition of alcoholic drink."[8]

Volstead's colleagues were divided as well. A few were less than congressionally cordial. In August 1921, the new Congressional Country Club invited every congressman to join. It was reported that several would refuse unless Representative Volstead declined his membership. The *New York Times* speculated on their reasoning: "Perhaps Mr. Volstead is too dry . . . There has never been any suggestion that he uses, or used, liquor himself. Will the Congressional Country Club exclude gentlemen who voted for prohibition, though they didn't believe in it, in the firm confidence that they themselves would always be able to get what they want when they wanted it? If it does, there will be no club. Mr. Volstead, it would seem, has committed the gravest possible offense against the Congressional code of etiquette: he has been sincere. No wonder he is blackballed."[9]

Violent criticism extended to the halls of Congress. Senator James A. Reed of Missouri attacked Volstead on the Senate floor, likening him to some of the worst persons in history: "I said that I should like to see the man who would vote against the Constitution of his own country. I have discovered that man and I have described him . . . I see in Mr. Volstead's face the countenances of those who have led in the fanatical crusades, the burning of witches, the executioners who applied the torch of persecution, and I saw them all again today when I looked at the author of this bill." Volstead's colleagues in the House voted 181 to 2 (out of 435 members) to ask the Senate to formally censure Reed.[10]

Minnesota congressman Andrew J. Volstead received hate mail and even death threats for writing Prohibition's enforcement law.

The next year Representative G. H. Tinkham of Massachusetts brought a resolution to the floor of the House attacking Volstead's integrity and calling for him to resign as Judiciary Committee chair. Tinkham accused Volstead of taking contributions from the Anti-Saloon League, asking "whether or not a private organization participating actively in elections with legislation in view shall be allowed to spend money for or subsidize members of Congress in advance of their action upon such legislation." The House members shouted down the bill and all but three supported Volstead. After the "turmoil" subsided, Volstead commented, "I have never shirked a fair fight but have always tried to treat my opponents fairly,

and, as a rule, I have in turn received fair treatment—although the fight over prohibition has at times been very bitter. The member from Massachusetts who poses as one of the prominent leaders of the wets is the only one in the House who has broken the rules of civilized warfare."[11]

After his 1922 reelection defeat, Volstead stayed in Minnesota. He practiced law and was a legal advisor to the head of the National Prohibition Enforcement Bureau's division for Minnesota, western Wisconsin, and the Dakotas.

By the time of the 1933 repeal, Volstead, ten years out of office, chose not to comment on the law that put his name in the lexicon of American history. "If I were to say that prohibition had been a mistake, there would be an awful uproar. And if I defended prohibition the other side would be after me. I have had experience enough to know that anything I say will be broadcast widely." Volstead wanted no part in any Prohibition postmortems. He continued to practice law in Granite Falls surrounded by the law books he used before he was elected to Congress in 1903. As to Prohibition, he told the *New York Times,* "I'm not even a spectator."[12]

HONEST ABE SUNDAE

1 large scoop vanilla ice cream

3 tablespoons chocolate syrup, warmed

2 tablespoons chopped dates

2 tablespoons chopped dried figs

Put the ice cream in a tall sundae glass. Cover with the warmed chocolate syrup and sprinkle with dates and figs.

SYRUPS AND FIXINGS

THE VALUE OF TOPPINGS
FOR VANILLA ICE CREAM

In a great many smaller communities the soda fountain man is "Put to it" to devise variations in ice cream dishes for his patrons. He probably can afford to keep on hand one kind of ice cream and naturally this is vanilla—it is "one grand flavor"—but he can offer manifold variations of sundaes by varying the toppings he puts on them.

NORTHWEST DRUGGIST, FEBRUARY 1921

Don't Care Syrup

When this recipe was published in 1915, the temperance movement was gaining strength. Communities were electing to "go dry" and not serve any alcoholic beverages. The name and ingredients suggest that not everyone agreed.

1 ounce (2 tablespoons) California brandy
¼ cup pineapple syrup
¼ cup vanilla syrup

Combine the ingredients in a half-pint jar and use within 2 or 3 days. Enough for 8 ice cream sodas or sundaes.

RECIPE NOTE: EASY SAMPLING SYRUPS

Commercially made flavoring syrups can be found in grocery stores and in specialty markets as well as online. They are shelf stable and, once opened, will last for months. And there are recipes on the Web for making your own flavored syrups. These usually need to be refrigerated and last only a few days or weeks.

But why invest the time, money, and shelf space in a row of bottles or make pints of flavored syrups when all you need is an ounce or two to see if you like a particular beverage or soda? The following technique quickly combines simple syrup with easily found concentrated flavors so you can set up your own soda fountain for an afternoon of treats. Some use frozen juice concentrates: just scoop out a tablespoon and return the container to the freezer. Others use popular jellies or ice cream topping flavors. If you decide not to make more flavored syrups, you can use these ingredients for their original purposes.

You will need to make your own simple syrup base. The recipe is easy to follow, and the result keeps for a very long time in the refrigerator. Measure out a quarter cup and add a bit of flavoring and you are ready to re-create the tasty beverages and ice cream treats of the 1920s.

Basic Simple Syrup

2 cups water
2 cups sugar

In a medium saucepan, combine the water and the sugar. Stir and cook over low heat until the sugar is fully dissolved. Take care that you don't have any stray sugar crystals on the side of the pan. Store in the refrigerator in a glass or plastic jar until ready to flavor and use.

Easy Sampling Syrups

For Ginger Syrup: simmer ¼ pound peeled, thinly sliced fresh ginger in 2 cups syrup for 5 minutes. Remove ginger and store any leftover syrup in the refrigerator.

For Vanilla Syrup: simmer half a fresh, split vanilla bean in 1 cup syrup for 5 minutes. Remove the bean and store any leftover syrup in the refrigerator.

For Juice-Based Syrups (grape, lemon, lime, orange, pineapple): mix 1 tablespoon of frozen juice, lemonade, or limeade concentrate into ¼ cup simple syrup.

For Jelly-Based Syrups (grape, mint, peach, raspberry, strawberry, wild cherry): put ¼ cup simple syrup in a microwavable container, add a tablespoon of jelly, and melt together at low power in 15-second increments.

For Champagne or Coffee Syrup: follow the directions for Basic Simple Syrup, substituting nonalcoholic white wine or coffee for the water.

A NEW AMERICAN TRADITION

"Sodas and sundaes are as much a part of our American life as telephones and newspapers. The widening spread of the temperance movement and the year-round stability to trade that is a part of the luncheonette department are both factors that will count for the soda fountain[']s great growth and prosperity during the years before us." —The Dispenser's Formulary or Soda Water Guide, 1915

Hot Chocolate Fudge Sundae Sauce

Delicious bittersweet sauce.

2 cups sugar
¼ cup cocoa powder
⅓ cup water, plus 2 tablespoons cold water
1 teaspoon cornstarch
½ cup heavy cream
1 teaspoon vanilla extract

In a heavy 2-quart pot, mix sugar and cocoa. Gradually stir in the ⅓ cup water and cook over medium heat, stirring occasionally, until the mixture reaches the soft ball stage, 235 to 240 degrees F, measured on a candy thermometer. Mix the cornstarch with the 2 tablespoons cold water. Stir into the hot chocolate mixture. Simmer a few more minutes to be certain the cornstarch is cooked, then set aside to cool. When the mixture has cooled to room temperature, stir in the heavy cream and vanilla. Mixture will keep in the refrigerator for up to a week. Warm the sauce over low heat on the stove, stirring frequently, before pouring over scoops of ice cream. Makes about 1¼ cups of sauce.

Cherry Royal Sauce

Folks could make this alcoholically fortified sauce even during Prohibition using port wine they'd legally set aside in their cupboard or cellar.

2 cups water

1 (14-ounce) can pie cherries, drained and chopped, or ½ pound fresh, tart red cherries, pitted and roughly chopped

3 cups sugar

¼ cup port wine

In a medium saucepan, combine the water and cherries. Simmer until the cherries are very tender, about 20 minutes. (Canned cherries will cook more quickly.) Carefully puree in a blender or food processor. For a smoother sauce, press through a medium sieve with a wooden spoon and discard any coarse bits of cherry skin remaining in the sieve. Return cherry puree to the saucepan and add the sugar. Simmer over medium heat, stirring until the sugar is dissolved. Reduce the heat to low and cook until the sauce is reduced by half. Cool, and then add the wine. Sauce will keep in the refrigerator for about a week or can be frozen. Makes about 2 cups.

> ## ELEGY WRITTEN IN A DESERTED BAR-ROOM
>
> Ice cream cones and candy
> Are preferred by Sue and Nan
> But as a substitute for whiskey
> They are not worth a d—
>
> AUTHORSHIP CENSORED
> *THE SODA FOUNTAIN,* AUGUST 1921

ABOUT THE SODA FOUNTAIN TRADE IN 1925

"Soda sales in the United States have grown to the astonishing total of $497,500,000 . . . Competition for this business is keen for there are 91,241 real soda fountains in the country, giving an average daily sales of $46.10 per fountain. Over forty thousand fountains—nearly half of the total—are in confectionery and soda shops; 38,503 are in the drug trade; over 7,000 in department, general and five and ten cent stores . . . All these fountains are distributed throughout the entire country pretty much in proportion to the population . . .

"These are interesting and significant figures, and it is a wise thing for a fountain man once in a while to sit down and study his market so as to judge more wisely his opportunities. It is an encouraging feeling for the man of energy and ambition to learn that of all the fountains in the country there are a 'best third' 33,510 to be exact—which do nearly three-quarters of the business and have an average daily sale of $91.40. It is a very tangible and attainable ambition to put your fountain into the class of the elite fountains, and here is a practical and convenient yardstick for measuring your trade accomplishments . . .

"Competition is keen in the fountain trade . . . There are three factors in the success of a fountain store—quality, sanitation, and service . . . The public is sensitive in the matter of its beverages and is becoming more and more discriminating in its tastes. The pure-food campaigns, the wide-spread propaganda for sanitation and hygiene, and the growing enlightenment of the people are all reflected in the demand at the soda fountain . . . the soda fountain which acquires and maintains a reputation for quality and purity automatically enjoys a profitable popularity." —"The Dispenser's Formulary," *Soda Fountain Magazine,* 1925

Christmas Dressing

½ cup raisins

½ cup dates

¼ cup citron (a candied peel found in the fruitcake ingredients section during holiday season)

½ cup prunes

1 cup Basic Simple Syrup (page 41)

Finely chop all the fruits. Put the syrup in a medium saucepan over medium heat. Add the chopped fruits and simmer for about 5 minutes, until the dried fruits plump up a bit. Cool and store in the refrigerator for up to a week. Makes about 2½ cups of sauce.

Summer Salad Topping

1 cup chopped fresh orange sections or 1 (8-ounce) can mandarin oranges, drained

1 (8-ounce) can crushed pineapple in juice, drained

½ cup crushed peeled, pitted peaches

½ cup crushed pitted cherries

Combine the fruits. Store the topping in the refrigerator for up to 3 days. Serve over fresh peach ice cream topped with whipped cream. Makes about 3 cups of topping.

THE SODA FOUNTAIN MAN

"You meet very few men with skill like that of the soda fountain expert. He takes a six-ounce glass and draws just one ounce of Coca-Cola syrup—the precise draw for the best drink service that eliminates waste. Done quickly? You bet. The rising bubbles just have time to come to a bead that all but o'ertops the brim as the glass is passed over the marble fountain for the first delicious and refreshing sip."
—Coca-Cola advertisement, June 1921

Pineapple-Marshmallow Dressing

½ cup pineapple syrup

½ cup marshmallow crème

Stir the syrup into the crème. Store in the refrigerator for up to 3 days.

Baltimore Cream

3 tablespoons peach syrup

½ cup orange syrup

⅓ cup vanilla syrup

½ cup strawberry syrup

heavy cream

carbonated water

Combine the syrups. The mixture will keep indefinitely in the refrigerator.

To make Baltimore Cream: put 1 tablespoon syrup in a 10-ounce glass. Stir in 1 teaspoon cream. Fill the glass with carbonated water. Recipe makes enough syrup for about 15 drinks.

NOTE: See page 6 for tips for using carbonated water.

"'Dry' time is ice cream time everywhere."

THE INTERNATIONAL CONFECTIONER, SEPTEMBER 1919

DESPERATE DAYS

"The drug store clerks' union is aiming at the vitals of the modern drug store, its heart and lungs—the candy counter and the soda fountain! With what diabolical cleverness they have waited till the nation leaned most heavily on their sustaining counters in the dry days of prohibition. Well they know that the public is dependent upon them for the very elements of life, for nourishment, for stimulation. The soda fountain and its adjacent candy counter are the town pump, the tavern, the corner grocery, and the sewing circle of days gone by. The very fabric of our social and political life is woven here. Can the nation support this final blow?" —Undated editorial in the *New York Evening Sun*

Chop Suey

1 cup Basic Simple Syrup (page 41)
2 cups crushed strawberries
1 (8-ounce) can crushed pineapple in juice, drained
3 ounces (1 cup loosely packed) shredded coconut
3 ounces (¾ cup) chopped walnuts

Combine syrup, strawberries, and pineapple. This mixture will keep in the refrigerator for a week. Stir in the coconut and walnuts just before serving as a topping for ice cream.

Tutti Frutti

1 cup cherry syrup

1 (8-ounce) can crushed pineapple in juice, drained

¼ cup crushed strawberries

¼ cup finely chopped pitted cherries

¼ cup crystallized ginger, finely chopped

2 ounces (½ cup) chopped walnuts

1 ounce (¼ cup) chopped pistachios

2 ounces (½ cup) chopped pecans

Combine the syrup, pineapple, strawberries, cherries, and ginger. This mixture can be kept in the refrigerator for up to a week. Stir in the nuts just before serving as a topping for ice cream.

OLD HABITS DIE HARD

"Bar Ex-Patrons not welcome. The trouble is that the reformed 'bar flies' still retain their social habits long indulged at the corner saloon. At about the most crowded part of the day they enter his store, and ordering a glass of soda, proceed to lean their elbows on the counter and indulge in political or business gossip by the half hour." —"Learn Soft Drink Etiquette," *The Soda Fountain*, March 1931

Mexican Peanut Topping

This combination is especially good over chocolate ice cream.

⅓ cup sugar
⅓ cup hot black coffee
2 rounded tablespoons peanut butter

In a small bowl, add the sugar to the coffee and stir until is it fully dissolved. Carefully stir in the peanut butter with a fork or whisk. Store unused topping in the refrigerator for up to 3 days. Makes about ¾ cup topping.

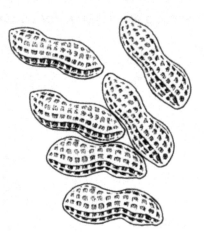

If they bring the ice cream into drug stores in kegs instead of tins, they will make a lot of men seem more at home.

WILL ROGERS, *THE COWBOY PHILOSOPHER ON PROHIBITION*

Coffee Caramel Topping

¼ pound vanilla caramels (about 9 caramels)
½ cup hot black coffee
1 cup heavy cream

In a small saucepan, add the caramels to the hot coffee. Cook over very low heat, stirring often, until the caramels melt. Cool, and then stir in the heavy cream. Store unused topping in the refrigerator for up to 3 days.

Nectar Punch

¼ cup lemon syrup
¼ cup strawberry syrup
¼ cup orange syrup
ice cream or carbonated water

Mix all syrups and store in a tightly covered container in the refrigerator for up to a week. To serve, pour over ice cream or mix 2 tablespoons with 8 ounces carbonated water.

It will take some men two years solid rehearsing
to learn how to order a soft drink without blushing.
WILL ROGERS, *THE COWBOY PHILOSOPHER ON PROHIBITION*

Opportunists, Scofflaws, and Bootleggers

"The problem of securing effective enforcement is one of some difficulty, but we are making substantial progress, and there is every reason to believe that public sentiment is steadily growing in favor of the law and that with the growth of such sentiment will come more effective and successful administration of its provisions."

"Volstead Claims Credit," *New York Times*, February 24, 1922

DESPITE CONGRESSMAN VOLSTEAD'S optimism and the best efforts of a decade of hardworking justice and treasury department officials, the ideals of Prohibition were pummeled by the reality of underfunded enforcement of a law that significant segments of the population held to be unfair. Although several states were dry before the Eighteenth Amendment was passed and ratified, the urban areas along the coasts and the Great Lakes had still enjoyed a robust, alcohol-fueled lifestyle that brought substantial excise tax dollars into the national treasury. In 1910, before federal income taxes were the law of the land, the federal government raised more than $200 million from alcohol-based taxes—about 30 percent of all federal revenue. With Prohibition, that source of revenue was gone. World War I–era federal income tax rates dropped, too. During the war the highest tax rate was 77 percent, levied against those with more than a million dollars in

taxable income. After the war, the highest rate dropped to a mere 24 percent.[1]

Like Volstead, John F. Kramer, the first federal Prohibition commissioner, was optimistic about the powers of enforcement. He felt "that the combined forces of prohibition and internal revenue could keep on [illicit liquor traffickers'] trail as long as Congress authorized employment of men for that purpose." When Commissioner Kramer left the office after only a year, however, he noted that it "will require some time and a great deal of effort to make conditions as they should be."[2]

Federal money was tight. Initially the government tried a "luxury tax" of one cent on every ten cents or portion thereof spent on a wide range of nonessentials—including ice cream and other soda shop treats. But the picture of youngsters having to find another penny for a dime cone was so unpopular that the category was eliminated in 1922. Fines and penalties had been expected to pay for enforcement, but they fell well short of the amount needed for serious efforts, bringing in a low of $2.3 million in 1922 and a high of $7.3 million in 1929. One estimate of the aggregated enforcement costs early in the Prohibition era came to far more than that. In 1922, according to William H. Anderson, state superintendent of the Anti-Saloon League, $100 million was spent annually for federal, state, and local Prohibition enforcement. The Census Bureau reported in 1927 that the states had contributed a mere $698,855 over the previous eight years of enforcement efforts.[3]

There was hope that the states would share equally in enforcement. After all, Section 2 of the Eighteenth Amendment directed that "The Congress and the several States shall have concurrent power to enforce this article by appropriate legislation." With concurrent power comes concurrent responsibility. Commissioner Kramer highlighted the problem, saying that Prohibition had been to some degree "forced upon whole states and especially upon large cities in which people had no sympathy whatever with the idea; in fact they scarcely knew what the term prohibition meant."[4]

The difficulty of finding incorruptible people and paying them continued throughout Prohibition. Mabel Willebrandt, assistant attorney general in charge of Prohibition enforcement, summed it up when she left office after more than seven years of effort: "Prohibition will never be successfully enforced from Washington alone. It simply cannot be done. It is local option and vigilance that will bring about effectiveness in the districts throughout the country."[5]

So when it came to enforcing the Volstead Act, the various state and federal

Up-to-date soda shop operators stood ready to provide tasty beverages and ice cream treats efficiently served from their modern, hygienic fountains.

agencies passed the buck while the coffers were bare. An analysis written in 1931 noted that enforcement "was set in motion in the halls of Congress by a dry majority which had at all times ample power to multiply its appropriations but consistently refused to act."[6]

Adding to the law enforcement woes were two major loopholes in the law.

First, the Eighteenth Amendment was very specific. It prohibited "manufacture, sale, and transportation of intoxicating beverages." But if you had a cellar full of wine or whiskey, you were free to drink all you wanted and to even share a glass with friends in your own home.

Second, the "cider exemption" allowed people to make alcoholic beverages. If not for this accommodation to the nation's farmers, once the supply of legally stored alcoholic beverages in individuals' cabinets and basements had been consumed, the United States would have been bone dry—not a drop of beverages with more than a half percent alcoholic content to be found anywhere—legally. During deliberations over the enforcement act, House member from Illinois "Uncle Joe" Cannon put it this way: "You can't enforce a law that seeks to prevent a man from making a barrel of cider, putting it down in his cellar and drinking it."

Representative Edward W. Pou of North Carolina, a conservative dry, agreed: "We are going too far when we say a housewife can't make blackberry wine or cider

Local police and G-men discover how Monday morning's washtub became part of the necessary equipment for Saturday's home-brew liquor making.

at her home. We must have some respect for public sentiment. The American people at least believe they were free. We had better come back to our senses and pass a bill that can be enforced."[7]

So, to placate the nation's farmers, who might just have a barrel of apple juice sitting out in the barn that might just ferment and develop an alcoholically "harder" kick all on its own, the act allowed anyone to make up to two hundred gallons of fruit juice–based beverages "for their own use" each year without paying attention to, or controlling, the alcoholic content. This exemption was further defined by a ruling from the Internal Revenue Bureau, precursor to the Internal Revenue Service. Following the spirit of the Eighteenth Amendment, such home brewers were allowed to "manufacture non-intoxicating cider and fruit juices." The decision defined the critical term—*non-intoxicating*—specifying it to mean "non-intoxicating in fact, and not necessarily less than one-half of one per cent of alcohol as provided in Section 29 of Title II of the said act."[8]

California grape growers, many of whom had initially torn up their vineyards, began increasing their acreage. In 1919 growers had shipped 150,000 gallons of grape juice. In 1920 they shipped just about half a million gallons, a nearly 400 percent increase. They also shipped compressed cakes of dried grapes, skins, and stems, ready for rehydrating and, well, *fermenting* in farm sheds and city basements all around the country.

But not all grapes made their way into basement wineries. Far more of the crop satisfied those who delighted in soda fountain beverages. After scientists at the University of California perfected vacuum condensing, growers started shipping grape syrup—grape juice with the "water eliminated and the sugar retained. Destined to become popular both at the soda fountain and in the home." As Horatio F. Stoll, head of the California Grape Growers Association, wrote, "Necessity is the mother of invention but prohibition is the god father of the grape syrup industry." Recipes for grape sodas, grape sundaes, and grape ice cream populated the recommendations of soda fountain promoters.[9]

Sadly, for those who wanted "real" beer, the raised alcoholic content exemption did not apply to grain-based beverages. Beer could be homemade, but home brewers were limited to a half percent alcohol by volume, even if it was just for their own use.

And, individuals could sell their homemade wine or beer if they didn't exceed the half percent alcohol regulation. So how were sellers to know if they were within the law? *Popular Science* magazine had the answer. Under the headline "Measuring the Home-Brew Kick," author John Walker Harrington described methods and instruments to prevent the "terror of being a lawbreaker." Using them, the "householder can find scant excuse for pleading ignorance of the strength of the potions made under his roof."[10]

Home manufacturing was of interest to a few people, but a great many others sought quicker routes to alcoholic satisfaction. The round-ups reported in just one *New York Times* article published during the first year of the "dry decade" highlight the variety of scofflaw and bootlegging possibilities. Early on in Prohibition, on November 24, 1922, the *Times* described two speakeasies, bootleg activity at a pharmacy, and rum-running.

Entry into the "Sailor's Den" near the Navy Yard operated on code: "The place was in a sub-cellar. Five raps get a prospective customer by the front door. Then if he holds up three fingers he is allowed to proceed to the second door, where the raising of two fingers is a sign that he is all right."

A Brooklyn soda fountain offered more than it advertised: "Adam Grodski did not live up strictly to the sign in front of his place, the agent said. This sign said 'soft drinks only.'" After being stuffed with soft drinks, the agents persuaded the owner to get them a round of Scotch whisky, which he obtained by calling up a dumbwaiter in the rear.

Although alcohol could be prescribed by physicians for genuine illnesses, some drugstores operated more freely. As the *Times* reported, the undercover agent purchased a pint of whisky from a pharmacy owned by Bernhardt Handt. Leaving the drugstore, the agent saw the opportunity for more enforcement action as he noticed an automobile which had stopped in front of the place. He searched the car and said he found five cases of Scotch whisky and a fifteen-gallon cask of alcohol.

Where did the bootleg whisky, rum, and other spirits come from? Much of it was imported from ships slipping into shore under cover of darkness. The same *Times* story provided details: "Five schoo-ners believed to be rum-runners which have been off Atlantic City for several days were reported last night by coast guards to have disappeared. It was believed that the schooners had evaded the guards and slipped into one of the many small havens along the Jersey coast."

The coast guards in Cape May, New Jersey, would appeal to headquarters for faster patrol boats as the result of such evasions. But getting speedy boats and other Prohibition reinforcements was a problem all across the country.

As the dry decade continued, Prohibition officers spent "their energy upon the sale of alcoholic drinks in public places and by bootleggers." There they found opportunities in the thousands. And, by the end of the era, alcohol consumption had dropped. A *Times* article in 1929 claimed that "Prohibition has very materially reduced both the production and consumption of intoxicating liquors throughout the United States." *Popular Science* reported some specifics: "Drinking gives the average American an annual dose of a little over four tenths of a gallon as compared with the pre-prohibition record of about one and seven tenths gallons." After Prohibition was repealed, it would take four decades—until 1970—for people to start drinking as much per capita as the nation did before Prohibition.[11]

Other consumption practices changed dramatically, too. Soda shop delights stepped in to quench the nation's thirst. Again, the *New York Times* reported the story: in 1929 "Americans spent $700,000,000 annually at soda fountains and the amount is increasing at the rate of $250,000,000 more each year, representing a little more than 2 per cent of the country's retail trade."[12]

After Prohibition was repealed, tax revenues went up, too. In that first year, the federal government collected $258,911,332 in taxes on alcohol, or nearly 9 percent of total federal revenue. Some might say, for good or ill, happy days were here again.[13]

SODA COCKTAIL

freshly squeezed juice of ½ lemon

1½ ounces lemon syrup

½ ounce champagne syrup

few dashes angostura bitters

dash orange bitters

⅓ cup shaved ice

carbonated water, 6 ounces,
    approximately

Combine all the ingredients in a cocktail shaker and shake thoroughly. Strain into a 10-ounce glass.

ICE CREAM SODA WITH A "KICK"

John Barleycorn just will not stay dead. His latest resurrection appears to be in Philadelphia where ice cream soda with a kick in it is the specialty of a number of sources. The cat was let out of the bag by Miss Winetta L. Stacks, superintendent of the Philadelphia Deaconess Home, who said that orphan boys at the home had been getting ice-cream sodas and exhibiting prize jags a short time later. She said Federal agents had wiped out at least one place where the jazzy sodas were sold.

THE SODA FOUNTAIN, MAY 1921

"DRY" FRUIT AND SYRUP BEVERAGES

CASH IN ON PROHIBITION

Wake up to the fact that the money formerly
spent for alcohol as it went over the bar can
be diverted very easily to the cash registers
behind the soda fountain and the candy counter.
Now—is the time to realize that the public wants
well served drinks and a place where it gets good
merchandise and quick service for its money.
The saloon did not only cash in on a place for
serving liquors, but it cashed in on the fact
that it became a meeting place. And that is the
main point to develop in your trade.

BERT KAHNWEILER, *COMMON SENSE DRUG STORE ADVERTISING* 1921

THE WONDERS OF GOPHER PRAIRIE

"A drug store with a soda fountain that was just huge, awful long, and all lovely marble; and on it there was a great big lamp with the biggest shade you ever saw—all different kinds of color glass stuck together, and the soda spouts, they were silver and they came right out of the bottom of the lampstand! Behind the fountain there were glass shelves and bottles of new kinds of soft drinks, that nobody ever heard of. Suppose a fella took you there!" —Bea Sorenson in *Main Street* by Sinclair Lewis

Five O'Clock Tea

⅓ cup strong iced tea
⅓ cup tart lemonade
⅓ cup ginger ale
crushed ice
orange slice and mint for garnish

Combine liquids in a 12-ounce glass and add crushed ice. Garnish with slice of fresh orange and sprig of fresh mint.

To make a pitcher:
3 cups strong iced tea
3 cups tart lemonade
2 (12-ounce) bottles ginger ale
3 cups crushed ice

Mix the tea and lemonade in a large (4-quart) pitcher. Just before serving stir in the ginger ale and crushed ice.

Grape Juice Highball

1 ounce ginger syrup
1 ounce orange syrup
shaved ice
4 ounces grape juice, approximately

Put the syrups in a 10-ounce glass. Add about a half cup shaved ice. Fill with grape juice and stir.

AS YOU PROBABLY KNOW, OLD PAL

Water is a wondrous blessing
Good for washing necks and ears,
Just the thing for making rivers
And surrounding ships and piers,
Nice to park beneath the bridges
Swell for making rain and ink
Water is a wondrous blessing,
But it makes a helluva drink.

JOSEPH PATRICK MCEVOY, *THE SWEET DRY AND DRY*

THE BOOTLEGGER'S OVERHEAD

"On the first of next month I'll be winding up my business in New York . . . Then I'll kiss booze peddling good-by and go while the going is good. I have been one of the small fry . . . my earnings figure like this. By the time you sell it in New York . . . the stuff has cost you about sixty dollars a case [including] as regular graft on the way, ten dollars a case. The chauffeur on the truck draws $100 a week and the two guards from seventy-five to $100. You sell it for about ninety dollars a case if it is bulk delivery, or about ninety-five dollars if you drop it in small lots. In the March slump, after people had just paid their income taxes and felt poor, it fell to eighty-eight dollars. But ninety dollars is a fair average. That's thirty dollars a case clear profit, or $1500 for a fifty-case lot, provided everything has gone well.

"Of course your staff can't turn strait round and do it again. It is hard work, and both the chauffeur and the guards have been on edge every minute of the run. You must rest them a day or two in New York and a day or two in Canada. Then there are other delays, like weather and uncertain help. Guards and chauffeurs are always getting drunk or quitting on you and you have to rustle round for new men. Month in and month out a truck will make less than one round trip a week. But even at that if the importer has the luck not to bump anything he ought to average $1000 a week, even allowing for deterioration of his cars. His investment is just a truck, a touring car, and his current load." —An anonymous bootlegger, "Inside the Bottle," *Saturday Evening Post*, May 27, 1922

1921 Highball

2 ounces raspberry vinegar
¾ cup ice-cold ginger ale

Combine in an 8-ounce glass and stir.

Prohibition Sour

"A drink for men."

1 ounce lemon syrup
⅓ ounce orange syrup
freshly squeezed juice of ½ lime
crushed ice
carbonated water, 6 ounces, approximately

Put the syrups and lime juice in a 12-ounce glass. Add a scoop of crushed ice. Fill with carbonated water and stir.

I knew one man in a dry town when he took his first Grape Juice Highball; it took three Doctors to revive him.

WILL ROGERS, *THE COWBOY PHILOSOPHER ON PROHIBITION*

HISTORY OF THE LIME RICKEY

The rickey was created by bartender George A. Williamson at a Washington, DC, bar, Shoomakers, at the end of the nineteenth century. Lobbyist Colonel Joe Rickey would come into the bar to have his "mornin's morning," a beverage of bourbon, ice, and Apollinaris sparkling water. According to legend, one day another patron asked for "one of those Joe Rickey drinks, but put a lime in it." Over time the liquor component changed from bourbon to gin. Shoomakers changed, too. With DC prohibition in place in 1917, the bar tried shifting to softer beverages, but the newspaper reporters, politicians, and lobbyists who made up its clientele found satisfaction elsewhere. After fifty-five years in business, the bar closed in 1918.

Raspberry Rickey

1½ ounces raspberry syrup
¼ teaspoon raspberry vinegar
½ fresh lime
crushed ice
carbonated water, 6 ounces, approximately
fresh raspberries for garnish

Combine the syrup and vinegar in a 12-ounce glass. Squeeze the lime juice into the glass and then drop in the lime shell. Add a large spoon of crushed ice, and fill with carbonated water. Mix with a tall spoon and decorate with fresh raspberries.

Minted Pineapple Rickey

1¼ ounces pineapple syrup

½ ounce crème de menthe syrup

½ fresh lime

crushed ice

carbonated water, 6 ounces, approximately

mint or orange slice for garnish

Combine the syrups in a 12-ounce glass. Squeeze the lime juice into the glass and then drop in the lime shell. Add a large spoon of crushed ice, and fill with carbonated water. Mix with a tall spoon and decorate with fresh mint or orange slice.

THE CHOICE BETWEEN "EX-SALOONS" AND SODA FOUNTAINS

"The ex-saloon, as a usual thing, has no soda fountain. It deals entirely in near beer, bottled drinks, sandwiches, gambling devices of one sort and another, and salted peanuts. The proprietors as a general rule, have scoffed at the soda fountains but the soda fountains are getting the trade nowadays. The patrons of the ex-saloons and of the modern fountains cannot help noting the difference and being impressed by the dinginess of the ex-saloon." —The Soda Fountain, August 21, 1921

Jitney Julep

½ ounce pineapple syrup
½ ounce mint syrup
1 ounce grape juice
shaved or crushed ice
carbonated water, 6 ounces, approximately

In a 12-ounce glass, combine the syrups and grape juice. Add ice, and fill with carbonated water. Stir to combine.

PROHIBITION PROFITS

"But just think of the money Prohibition puts in a man's pocket," said the good deacon. "That's right," agreed the unregenerate backslider. "An ice-cream soda only costs about five times as much as a glass of beer used to."

"PHILADELPHIA RECORD," THE SODA FOUNTAIN, MARCH 1921

Summer High Ball

1 small scoop lemon water ice (Italian ice)
1 ounce lemon syrup
1 ounce vanilla syrup
¾–1 cup ginger ale

Into a 12-ounce glass scoop the lemon ice, then add the syrups and top with the ginger ale. Stir briefly and serve with a tall spoon and straw.

Bliss High Ball

1 ounce ginger ale syrup
carbonated water, 6 ounces, approximately
1 small scoop lemon water ice (Italian ice)

In a 12-ounce glass, combine ginger ale syrup and carbonated water. Gently float the scoop of lemon ice on top. Serve with a tall spoon.

BRIGHT CHANGE ON MAIN STREET

"A complete revolution has been effected in the appearance of some towns by the substitution of the open windows of the ice cream parlor for the drawn blinds of the old saloon." —*The Soda Fountain*, April 1921

Klondike Fizz

¼ ounce orange syrup

½ ounce lemon syrup

1 ounce strawberry syrup

⅓ cup crushed ice

carbonated water, 6 ounces, approximately

orange slice or strawberry for garnish

Combine the syrups, ice, and water in a 12-ounce glass. Mix with a tall spoon and decorate with an orange slice or fresh strawberry.

Yankee Punch

1 ounce pineapple syrup
⅓ ounce raspberry syrup
freshly squeezed juice of ½ lemon
⅓ cup crushed ice
carbonated water, 6 ounces, approximately
fruit for garnish

Combine syrups, juice, ice, and water in a 12-ounce glass. Mix with a tall spoon and decorate with fresh fruit of your choice.

VOLSTEAD'S DRY WIT

Exchange reported from the floor of the House of Representatives.

The Republican leader reported that Mr. Volstead has an engagement Wednesday in Milwaukee as he sought to change the order of business for the next week.

"Reserving the right to object" said Representative Stafford, Republican of Milwaukee, "Does it mean that the distinguished author of the Volstead law hopes to be converted after going there?"

"Let us hope it is the people of Milwaukee who will be converted," Mr. Volstead replied.

"I pray not," Mr. Stafford shot back, and the House laughed.

"VOLSTEAD AMUSES HOUSE," *NEW YORK TIMES*, MAY 18, 1922

BOTTLERS CONTEMPLATE FANCIFUL DRINKS

"If America is to remain dry it will not be because of the lack of new non-alcoholic drinks. Following are some of the many names for beverages for which applications for registration as trade marks were applied for in Washington from May 30 to June 27: Cremo, Green Mountain, Grape Oka, Taxi-Cola, Choc-la, and Clearock." —The Spatula, July 1922

Watermelon Julep

2 cups seedless watermelon pulp
freshly squeezed juice and pulp of ⅓ lemon
freshly squeezed juice and pulp of ½ orange
¼–¾ cup sugar
2 cups very cold water
sprigs of mint for garnish

Process the watermelon in a blender or food processor. Add the citrus juice and pulp; pulse to combine. Add sugar to taste. Blend in the water, and place mixture in the freezer until it just begins to turn slushy. Scoop into a footed glass such as a sherbet dish or a margarita glass. Garnish with sprigs of mint.

Wild Cherry Bounce

1½ ounces wild cherry syrup
freshly squeezed juice of 1 lemon
⅛ cup crushed ice
carbonated water, 6 ounces, approximately
¼ cup crushed pitted cherries

In a 12-ounce glass, combine all the ingredients and stir until blended.

Cider Frappé

2 cups sweet cider
freshly squeezed juice of 1¼ oranges
freshly squeezed juice of ½ lemon
¼ cup sugar

Mix all the ingredients and freeze to a slush. Serve in a sherbet or margarita glass. Makes 4 (⅓-cup) servings.

HALLOWEEN CELEBRATION

"At last year's Hallowe'en party we had beer; this year it was cider."

"Oh, that was tough."

"No, it was hard!"

WHAT HAPPENED WHEN DETROIT WENT DRY

"All of the bugaboos of the 'wets' shouted from every platform and rostrum during the hot campaign which preceded Detroit's entry into the 'dry' column [in 1917] have failed to materialize and as far as the average man can see Detroit is hustling along as busily as ever, as prosperously as ever and apparently not missing old John Barleycorn to any marked degree.

"Detroit's big breweries are turning out soft drinks and hundreds of former saloons are selling them with ice cream, soda, candy and cigars, and doing a prosperous business." —The International Confectioner, February 1919

Ginger Tea

3 ounces (or ⅛ cup) iced tea
1 ounce simple syrup
1 ounce ginger ale syrup
carbonated water, 4 ounces, approximately
crushed ice
orange slice for garnish

Mix the tea, syrups, water, and ice in a 12-ounce glass. Serve with an orange slice for garnish.

Ginger Drake

From the Drake Hotel in Chicago.

1 ounce pineapple syrup
1 ounce lime syrup
carbonated water, 5 ounces, approximately
3 ounces ginger ale
crushed ice

Mix syrups, water, and ginger ale in a 16-ounce glass and add crushed ice to fill.

Ginger Juicer

1 ounce ginger syrup
1 ounce lime syrup
1 ounce white grape juice
carbonated water, 6 ounces, approximately
crushed ice

Mix syrups, juice, and water in a 16-ounce glass and add crushed ice to fill.

Suffragists, Saloons, and Soda Shops

Father, dear father, come home with me now!
The clock in the steeple strikes two;
The night has grown colder, and Benny is worse
But he has been calling for you.
Indeed he is worse[,] Ma says he will die,
Perhaps before morning shall dawn;
And this is the message she sent me to bring
"Come quickly, or he will be gone."
Come home! come home! come home!
Please, father, dear father, come home.

—Henry Clay Work

WOMEN HAD LONG BEEN SEEN to suffer most from the damaging effects of drink upon society. In Henry Clay Work's 1864 melodramatic "Song of little Mary standing at the bar-room door while the shameful midnight revel rages wildly as before," the tragedy awaiting the bar-habituating father worsens with each hourly stanza, until in the end his son, "little Benny[,] is dead and gone with the angels of light."[1]

By practice, if not by law, saloons were the domain of men. The Anti-Saloon League campaign fostered the image of husbands and fathers spending time and wages in bars, lending a kernel of truth to the song's saga. But by the turn of the century, women were starting to take action. Not everyone was ready to wield a hatchet and follow Carrie Nation on her liquor-smashing bar tour, but for more than a generation before the 1917 passage of the Eighteenth Amendment the pressure for prohibition and push for woman suffrage had been building. Finding their voices, women were ready to speak out on public issues. As prohibition moved across the country, suffragists marched with it. State after state enacted community local options or voted to go completely dry, and some even let women's votes help decide.

By 1917 twenty-three states had prohibition laws on the books and eighteen allowed women to vote in some, if not all, elections. The overlap between restrictions and rights reveals interesting sectional differences. Of the eighteen states where women had the right to vote, fifteen had also enacted some form of prohibition. Only the suffrage states of California, Illinois, and New York remained thoroughly wet. In most states, prohibition preceded suffrage; however, four western states—Colorado, Oregon, Washington, and Idaho—gave women the right to vote first, and in Arizona both measures became law in 1914. A dozen states, mostly in the south, went dry without enacting woman suffrage: Georgia, Mississippi, North Carolina, Tennessee, West Virginia, Virginia, Alabama, South Carolina, Montana, and—in New England—Maine and New Hampshire.

Business interests and individuals recognized, and possibly feared, the power in these joint concerns. In 1881 the National Brewers Congress adopted a resolution condemning woman suffrage. Two years after being defeated for reelection by Woodrow Wilson, President William Howard Taft wrote of woman suffrage and prohibition in the *Saturday Evening Post:* "the lack of experience in affairs and excesses of emotion on the part of women in reaching their political decisions upon questions of this kind are what would lower the average practical sense and self-restraint of the electorate in case they were admitted to it now."[2]

Dedicated, progress-seeking suffragists kept any connections with prohibition out of their public discussions. Activist Ida Husted Harper said, "We are in the midst of a [suffrage] campaign [in New York State]. We are not confusing this with the prohibition issue." In Chicago, where antiprohibition sentiments ran strong, Marion H. Drake ran for election

as alderman on a platform that included "free lunch and saloons." May Wright Sewall of Milwaukee addressed the connection directly: "Votes for women will no more prohibit drink than they will prohibit food."[3]

Andrew Volstead recognized the importance of women and women's votes to the long-term success of Prohibition,

Where corner saloons had been bastions for men only, the neighborhood soda shop offered delights for men, women, and families, changing the social dynamic of the era.

as he indicated in a 1921 Anti-Saloon League speech: "In most of the dry states prohibition came without the vote of the women; [but] since they have been given the ballot they have always been the foe of the saloon, they suffered the most from it, and they will never consent that it be restored."[4]

Although few women were able to vote to enact Prohibition, Andrew Volstead knew that once woman suffrage was achieved their support would continue to keep restrictions on liquor sales.

Women affected more than political movements, however: they were prized soda fountain customers. An article in the *Soda Fountain* explained, "The fountains that are conspicuous successes are patronized extensively by women. Women have long figured among the dispenser's best customers and for them he has concocted the most delicious and elaborate sundaes, the daintiest beverages, the most delicately flavored creams and ices. Such customers have also exerted a salutary influence upon the character of many shops, spurring the proprietor to greater endeavors to keep his place immaculately clean and to furnish them with delicacies which would appeal to their esthetic tastes."[5]

And, alas for Congressman Volstead's hope, as saloons disappeared, those who wanted to consume alcoholic beverages—both men and women—found ways to do it. Some began drinking openly in their homes, indulging in either homemade wines or precious high-spirited bottles purchased legally before January 20, 1920, and stashed for the duration. Others patronized the city speakeasy, a place described by reporter Russell Owen as accommodating to women customers: "Speakeasies to a large extent have followed a natural development determined by feminine emancipation." Here, as in the ice cream parlor, woman had a significant impact. Owen continued: "Speakeasies are seldom riotous places—the feminine influence is too strong . . . their greatest patronage is in the evening, drawing from the middle class."[6]

While some women enjoyed partaking of alcoholic beverages on the sly, others urged repeal of the Eighteenth Amendment. In 1928 Pauline Morton Sabin, a wealthy and well-connected New York socialite and activist, began her outspoken rejection of Prohibition. Once she had been a strong proponent, believing the law would lead to a safer life for her sons. But she had become disillusioned at the actual post-Prohibition temptations put before the nation's youth: "Girls a generation ago would not have ventured into a saloon. Today girls and boys drink at parties and then stop in speakeasies." In April 1929 Sabin resigned her position with the Republican National Committee to head the Women's Organization for National Prohibition Reform (WONPR), which quickly gathered followers nationwide. Sabin said, "The idea of our organization came from the number of letters we received from mothers across the country . . . It is a fact that young America is drinking far more than ever before."[7]

WONPR members took to the streets much as their mothers and sisters had for voting rights. Sabin explained, "Prohibition reform is logically a woman's cause, for national prohibition is the first Federal experiment in social legislation which has failed disastrously and brought in its wake social conditions which directly threaten youth and the home."[8]

Social and economic forces coalesced, and after a decade of controversy Prohibition was quickly repealed in 1933. Women had been involved in all facets of the reforms from start to finish, and they now enjoyed changes in the social structure relating to the modern world and the place of alcoholic beverages in it. As the *New York Times*'s Russell Owen concluded, "These changes make it certain that no drinking place can ever occupy the place that the old-fashioned saloon did. There is too much competition. The drinking place of the future will be co-educational."[9]

AMERICAN GIRL SUNDAE

1 large scoop vanilla ice cream

½ ounce grape juice

½ ounce orange syrup

marshmallow crème for topping

maraschino cherry for garnish

Put the ice cream in a tulip sundae glass. Mix the grape juice and orange syrup, and pour it over the ice cream. Top with a spoonful of marshmallow crème and then a maraschino cherry.

Business-boosting articles on how to manage soda shops suggested that hiring women to work behind the fountain could increase sales.

ICE CREAM SODAS AND BEVERAGES WITH MILK

THE INVENTION OF THE ICE CREAM SODA

During the Centennial Exposition in Philadelphia in 1876 drugstore clerk Robert M. Green was in charge of the soda fountain installed as one of the "new" attractions at the exposition. Green is credited with the invention of the ice cream soda. He bought a container of ice cream from a neighboring vendor so he could put a spoonful of the ice cream into a glass of fizzy soda water. Visitors to his stand were invited to step up and sample the drinks . . . the customers . . . liked it so well that they returned for additional orders of "that new mixture." Soon the fountain was crowded and Green had difficulty in securing a sufficient amount of ice cream.

"ICE CREAM SODA NEW DRINK," *THE SODA FOUNTAIN,* APRIL 1921

AN IDEAL ICE CREAM SODA

"First: take proper amount of syrup and sweet cream. (Note—no ice cream soda can be a perfect one without sweet cream.)

"Second: Coarse stream full force until the glass is nearly full.

"Third: Stir with a spoon which can be done without stirring out the [carbonation] enough to flatten the drink. Three or four brisk stirs with the spoon well down in the glass being careful not to break the layer of creamy foam on top, complete the mixing. We now have a glass of cream soda of the desired flavor, with a creamy foam on top.

"Fourth: Drop the scoop of ice cream in the center and finish with one or two quick squirts with fine stream near the edge of the glass." —C. H. Clark, *The Druggist Circular,* October 1919

CLASSIC ICE CREAM SODAS

Use these formulas with C. H. Clark's method, left, for an ideal ice cream soda. Mr. Clark specified the size of the scoop of ice cream by the # designation. The #20 scoop of ice cream means twenty scoops from a quart, or ⅜ cup. The #16 scoop means sixteen scoops from a quart, or ½ cup. The #10 scoop means ten scoops from a quart, or about ¾ cup. You can purchase ice cream scoopers by size. For these recipes I'll just call them small, medium, and large. As for the syrups or toppings, I think it is easier to measure them using the one-ounce jigger, but remember that one ounce is the same as two tablespoons, so two ounces would be the same as a quarter cup.

To make the sodas start with a 10-ounce soda glass with flared sides and add . . .

Chocolate: 2 ounces chocolate syrup, 2 ounces sweet cream, and a small scoop chocolate ice cream.

Strawberry: 1 ounce strawberry syrup, 1 ounce crushed strawberries, 2 ounces sweet cream, and a small scoop strawberry ice cream.

Vanilla: 2 ounces vanilla syrup, ¼ teaspoon vanilla extract, 2 ounces sweet cream, and a medium scoop vanilla ice cream.

Maple: 2 ounces real maple syrup, 2 ounces sweet cream, and a large scoop maple ice cream.

Pineapple: ¼ cup crushed pineapple, 1½ ounces pineapple syrup, 2 ounces sweet cream, and a small scoop vanilla ice cream.

Caramel: 2 ounces caramel syrup, 2 ounces sweet cream, and a small scoop caramel ice cream.

Nectar: 2 ounces Nectar Punch syrup (page 51), 2 ounces sweet cream, and a small scoop vanilla ice cream.

"No one as yet has been able to compute exactly how many sodas and sundaes the average American girl or boy can dispose of in the course of a day: probably too many."

AMERICAN DRUGGIST AND PHARMACEUTICAL RECORD, MAY 1919

"*IN DEFENSE OF THE SODA DISPENSER*"

"Soda dispenser must have ambition and gumption.

"There are many requirements that attach to the work of a soda dispenser. The ones cited are but a few. Yet these alone show that the lot of the successful soda dispenser is not an easy-go-lucky one in the fountain operated under modern conditions. The dispenser must have a good memory, he must be thorough. The dispenser goes out of his way to please you; he will make you feel welcome; he will make you want to come again . . . he will impel you to recommend the fountain where he is ready to serve to your friends, to other persons; he is building up good will for his employer." —The Soda Fountain, August 1922

Mexican Soda

⅓ ounce ginger syrup

⅓ ounce orange syrup

⅓ ounce pineapple syrup

1 small scoop vanilla ice cream

carbonated water, 6 ounces, approximately

In a 12-ounce soda glass, combine the syrups. Drop in the scoop of ice cream, and pour in carbonated water slowly down the side so that the soda will foam at the top.

Shamrock Delight

2 ounces crème de menthe syrup
½ ounce sweet cream
1 large scoop vanilla ice cream
carbonated water, 6 ounces, approximately
whipped cream for topping
sprigs mint, or crushed green Maraschino cherries, for garnish

In a 12-ounce soda glass, combine the syrup and cream. Drop in the ice cream, and pour in the carbonated water slowly down the side so that the soda will foam at the top. Garnish with whipped cream and sprigs of mint or crushed minted cherries.

HUMOROUS HISTORY LESSON

Year 1610—Indians sell Manhattan Island for a case of whiskey.

Year 1920—Citizens offer to swap it back.

THE SPATULA, MAY 1921

A DAY AT THE SODA FOUNTAIN

"Agile young men in jaunty white caps and uniforms lay out knife, fork, napkin, and glass of water with a single sweep of the hand. While through all murmurs of the fountain—the splash of syrup, the hum of the malted milk mixer and orange squeezer, the clicks of toaster and waffle irons, stock broker and stenographer lean contentedly against the counter over their accustomed bowls of cereal and cream.

"Mothers herd their plaintive offspring toward the glittering haven of the soda fountain for their midday meal of frankfurters and ice cream cones . . . Chauffeur and debutant, messenger boy and movie magnate meet in the great American fraternity of the sandwich and the chocolate ice cream soda.

"Three meals a day, once a function of hearth and home and lately of kitchenette and restaurant, are passing before our unconsidering gaze to the nickeled and marbled purlieus of the soda fountain.

"The soda fountain in the twentieth century is by way of becoming the great human filling station . . . set up at every strategic point . . . you can buy your favorite mixture of malted milk as you can buy your favorite gasoline from coast to coast.

"Indeed, in Tacoma or Tallahassee, if you listen with care, along the marble counter you may hear echoing the same cabalistic syllables of the soda man's code—the Esperanto of the trade—into whose mysteries the outside is seldom initiated. 'Burn one, let it cackle' is, for instance, the signal for an egg malted milk; 'draw one' for a cup of coffee, and 'black cow' for a chocolate milk. Everywhere the most familiar cry is 'chock in,' meaning chocolate ice cream soda." —Eunice Fuller Barnard, "Our Filling Station: The Soda Fountain," *New York Times,* February 2, 1930

Chocolate Flora Dora

1 medium scoop chocolate ice cream
3 tablespoons chocolate syrup
carbonated water, 6 ounces, approximately

In a 10-ounce soda glass, drop in ice cream. Top with syrup and fill with carbonated water.

Strawberry Flora Dora is made following above directions using strawberry ice cream and crushed strawberries.

Boston Coffee Ice Cream Soda

2 ounces coffee syrup
½ ounce sweet cream
carbonated water, 6 ounces, approximately
1 small scoop vanilla ice cream

In a 12-ounce soda glass, combine the syrup and cream. Add enough carbonated water to fill the glass three-quarters full. Drop in ice cream. Serve with long spoon and straw.

A Chocolate Bostonian is made by following above directions using Bostonian nut ice cream and chocolate sauce.

RECIPE NOTE: THE PARFAIT

A *parfait* is an ice cream mixture rather like a milk shake, meant to be eaten with a spoon. Some of these recipes originally called for mixing the ice cream, flavoring, and any liquid with an electric mixer or simply shaking them up. An immersion blender works really well, or use a regular blender. The ice cream mixes more easily if it is slightly softened.

Maple Pecan Parfait

1 large scoop maple ice cream, softened
⅓ cup heavy cream
¼ cup chopped pecans
whipped cream for topping

Combine the ice cream, cream, and pecans. Blend until smooth but not melted. Spoon into a tall glass, top with whipped cream, and serve with a spoon.

Cherry Parfait

1 large scoop vanilla ice cream, softened
½ cup crushed pitted cherries
¼ cup heavy cream
cherry for garnish

Combine the ice cream, pitted cherries, and cream. Blend until thick and smooth. Spoon into a tall glass, top with a large red cherry, and serve.

Orange Parfait

1 small scoop orange sherbet, softened
1 medium scoop vanilla ice cream,
    softened
¼ cup heavy cream
whipped cream for topping
strawberry for garnish

Combine the sherbet, ice cream, and heavy cream. Blend until thick and smooth. Spoon into a tall glass, top with whipped cream, and garnish with a strawberry.

Sober Americans: It is not in the humor of the American people to continue any type of fashion of drunkenness. The whole world is making for a sober world and America is leading the way.

RANDOLPH WELLFORD SMITH, *THE SOBER WORLD,* 1919

Coffee Milk Shake

1 ounce coffee syrup

1 ounce sweet cream

1 small scoop vanilla ice cream, softened

1 cup milk

nutmeg for garnish

Put syrup, cream, ice cream, and milk in a cocktail shaker and shake until thoroughly mixed. Pour into a glass, sprinkle nutmeg on top, and serve with a straw.

Superlative Milk Shake

¼ cup shaved or crushed ice

1 heaping tablespoon vanilla ice cream, softened

1 ounce milk

dash vanilla extract

3 teaspoons crushed fruit (berries are best)

1½ ounces grape syrup

carbonated water, 6 ounces, approximately

Combine all the ingredients except the carbonated water in a cocktail shaker and shake well. Transfer to a 10-ounce glass. Fill with carbonated water.

Frosted Chocolate

1 ounce (2 tablespoons) chocolate syrup
1 small scoop vanilla ice cream, softened
¼ cup crushed ice
carbonated water, 6 ounces, approximately
whipped cream or marshmallow crème for topping

Combine the chocolate syrup, ice cream, and crushed ice in a cocktail shaker. Shake until ice cream is dissolved, and pour into a 10-ounce glass. Fill with carbonated water. Top with whipped cream or marshmallow crème.

AL CAPONE BRANCHES OUT FROM BOOTLEGGING

Toward the end of the Prohibition era, Al Capone became a partner in a Chicago-area dairy. When he learned that the markup for milk was greater than that for beer or liquor and that the demand was universal he reportedly said, "Honest to God, fellas, we've been in the wrong racket right along."

ROBERT J. SCHOENBERG, *MR. CAPONE*

A FLAPPER'S APPEAL TO PARENTS

"If one judges by appearances, I suppose I am a flapper. I am within the age limit. I wear bobbed hair, the badge of flapperhood. (And, oh, what a comfort it is!) I powder my nose. I wear fringed skirts and bright colored sweaters, and scarfs, and waists with Peter Pan collars, and low-heeled 'finale hopper' shoes. I adore to dance. I spend a large amount of time in automobiles. I attend hops and proms, and ball-games and crew races and other affairs at men's colleges . . .

"I want to beg all you parents, and grandparents, and friends, and teachers, and preachers—you who constitute the 'older generation'—to overlook our short-comings, at least for the present, and to appreciate our virtues . . .

"'The war!' You cry. 'It is the effect of the war!' And then you blame prohibition. Yes! Yet it is you who set the example there! . . .

"Help us be worthy of the sacred trust that will be ours . . . Make your lives such an inspiration to us that we in our turn will strive to become an inspiration to our children and to the ages! Is it too much to ask?" —Ellen Wells Page in *The Outlook: An Illustrated Weekly Journal of Current Life*, December 6, 1922

Flapper Frappé

4 large ripe strawberries, chopped, plus 1 strawberry, sliced, for garnish
dash lemon juice
2 tablespoons heavy cream
carbonated water, 6 ounces, approximately
1 small scoop vanilla ice cream

Put the chopped strawberries in a 10- or 12-ounce tulip sundae glass. Add the lemon juice and mash. Stir in the cream. Add carbonated water to fill the glass halfway. Drop in the ice cream, and then fill the glass with more carbonated water, making sure to pour down the side and away from the ice cream. Serve with a sliced strawberry on top.

WORKING FOR BEAUTY AS WOMEN TAKE TO THE WORKPLACE

"Woman's personal appearance helps her to make and hold her place in the business world . . . Once upon a time the American girl may have done her own hair at her leisure with curl papers or curling iron, before her dresser mirror. But now her work day program must fit into the nation's high speed in industry so she utilizes the services of the specialist. She must be groomed.

"What are the hours, the working conditions, and the wage of the girl who plies the curling iron so skillfully to your locks? . . . Does the small tip you slip into her apron pocket help toward an ice cream sundae? Or does it mean actual bread and butter? . . . One girl in a small shop said she made 70 cents a day in that way." —"Young, Slim, and Nice Looking—How?" *Life and Labor Bulletin,* October 1921

American Girl Soda

"This makes a sweet drink and one containing the ingredients most popular with young girls, hence the name."

1 ounce chocolate syrup
⅛ ounce coffee syrup
¼ ounce vanilla syrup
1 ounce heavy cream
carbonated water, 6 ounces, approximately

In a 12-ounce glass, combine the syrups and cream. Stir with a spoon and then add the carbonated water, stirring to blend. Serve with a straw.

INNOVATION IN ICE CREAM FLAVORS AND DESIGN

"There is far more to the development of new sundaes and flavors than the layman might suppose," said a fountain expert. "Unless we keep adding fashions in frappes we are apt to find a falling off in our patronage . . . Three weeks were required to develop this [new tea] flavor . . . When we finally introduced tea ice cream sodas and sundaes, they met with a hearty reception at first, but after a month or so, consumer interest waned. Meanwhile we were working on another new extract. Occasionally, a novelty will become a staple through widespread acceptance, although this is infrequent. There are several important considerations that must be borne in mind in the formulating of a sundae or soda . . . Appearance is a factor that we must always keep in mind."—Bertram Reinitz "Soda Inventors are Ingenious," *New York Times*, March 4, 1928

Lincoln Frappé

1 ounce coffee syrup

⅛ ounce caramel syrup

⅛ ounce vanilla syrup

⅓ cup shaved or finely crushed ice, plus more for serving

⅓ cup heavy cream

carbonated water, 4 ounces, approximately

Combine flavoring ingredients, ice, and heavy cream in a cocktail shaker and shake. Strain into 12-ounce glass. Add carbonated water and plenty of additional shaved ice.

Modern Entertainment Builds Soda Business

DOING THINGS THAT PAY

"Even if you go no further than to call attention to the day by some placard at the fountains, some dish on the menu, some especial offering of ice cream, or some show case display, you will not have worked in vain, for whether sales show an immediate answer or not, you nevertheless will have created an opinion in the public mind that you are up-to-date . . . the community will turn their thoughts to your place."

Northwestern Druggist, February 1922

PROHIBITION-ERA SODA FOUNTAINS were palaces of modern, hygienic entertainment. Gone were the dust-trapping gewgaws of yesteryear. As saloons closed, soda fountain business increased significantly. No one behind the counter had time to spend an hour a day polishing fancy surfaces; instead, stylish white porcelain and marble were the ticket to up-to-date success.

Advertisements by the manufacturers of soda fountain counters and equipment touted efficient and sanitary features. One of the best on the market, the Walrus White Soda Fountain, was iceless and leakproof. Counters were nonabsorbent, were easy to clean, and wouldn't stain. Ice cream bins had "covers that slide backwards, easily, handily, out of the way." A "double cooling coil capacity" delivered on efficient cooling, as did "two separate and distinct heavy copper linings" to

keep the chambers cold. Practicality was the byword as the syrup and carbonated water pumps were durably made of "solid nickel silver, not plated."[1]

The attentive soda server was ready to present the customer with pleasing, refreshing choices. He quickly concocted any of a wide variety of ever-changing treats with names that delightfully reflected the times, if not the ingredients.

93

One soda fountain veteran recalled that, years earlier, "a soda fountain was built like a circus wagon. Carved and ornamented from one end to the other and . . . almost impossible to keep clean. The fountain of today, plain in design, is more beautiful and more sanitary." He continued, "In the old days the glamour of the fountain would sell anything. We gave them the best we had but that wasn't very good."[2]

Now, as business and competition increased and as tasty novelties attracted people's attention and satisfied their appetites, the situation was different and the opportunities practically limitless. Sundaes and sodas were named after events, holidays, famous people, travel destinations, or some whimsy of the soda man's imagination: "The American public is fond of a complicated drink which will appeal to the eye and is willing to pay for it. The profit for the inventor of any novelty which strikes the public taste is likely to be fabulous."[3]

In this modern era, finding the right soda fountain man was key to business success. Beyond the standard duties of scooping out ice cream and pouring sodas, the man who "does things out of the ordinary is the one that draws the crowd," observed the *Midland Druggist*. The skilled soda dispenser needed "ambition and gumption." His lot was not a "happy-go-lucky-one": his job was full of responsibility—he was the face of the business, not just some fellow jerking a few syrup and water handles.

With good equipment, tasty ingredients, and a well-trained, dedicated staff in place, go-getter soda fountain owners reached out to draw customers into their stores. Articles in soda and drugstore trade journals promoted fresh ideas, bringing newly developed scientific and psychological principals of national advertising campaigns home to Main Street. Writers gleaned insights from famed promotional practitioners such as John B. Watson, Daniel Starch, and Walter Dill Scott, whose work was legendary, and spun them into appeals designed to woo customers and bring them back time and again. The lesson, simply put, was this: "Advertise your fountain and your fountain will advertise you."[4]

Trade magazines offered endless ideas for the fountain men: Attract businessmen with specials. Serve ladies dainty sundaes; create special sodas. Invite high school students to write reviews. Gussy up hot cocoa and coffee with whipped toppings and extras. Cater to the movie-going crowd. Even become an entertainment center.

The time certainly was right. One entertainment draw was radio. In the first years of Prohibition, radio use fairly exploded across the nation. In June 1922, there were 378 stations on the air in 225 cites. Most were low wattage, reaching just a few miles. Hobbyist operators provided programming by playing Victrola records over the airwaves for their neighbors to tune in. Some listeners moved crystal set whisker wires to capture the signal, while others bought easy-to-operate radio sets. In 1922 sales of RCA "Radio Music Boxes" totaled $11 million.[5]

A savvy soda man could set up a "radio receiving station" in his fountain and attract patrons to come in and listen to programs. *Candy and Soda Fountain Profits* made it sound so easy: "The merchant . . . can build [business] wonderfully well for himself if he installs the first radio receiving set in his community. The operation of the modern receiving set is so simple that anyone can become expert at tuning-in after an hour or two spent in experimentation . . . By advertising daily concerts and by giving the radio prominent display in the store, there are trade-drawing and business-building possibilities galore."[6]

But times were changing quickly, and the entertainment potential changed with them. Sales of radio sets for home use totaled $50 million in 1924 and, importantly, a network of twenty-six stations linked coast to coast by AT&T cables carried news and nationally significant events to reach thousands of people across the country simultaneously. Radio was out of the hands of the hobbyists and under the control of broadcasters. Soda fountain operators needed to find a new cultural connection as more and more people simply stayed home and listened to the radio in their own front parlors.[7]

Motion pictures opened up a new and dynamic opportunity. Unlike with radio, people had to leave their homes to go to the movies, which at first were silent but boasted full sound by the middle of the Prohibition era. Dating couples or families out for an evening's fun could stop by the fountain on their way to or from the movies. There was plenty to talk about—newsreels, comedies, dramas, double features. And this inexpensive brand of entertainment left room in the budget for an ice cream soda or sundae on the way home. By 1933 "attendance at motion picture theaters has about tripled—the motion picture now occupies two hours or more of the average person's time each week." Wise fountain operators capitalized on this trend, too.[8]

From shiny fixtures to radio entertainment centers to movie-themed concoctions, business-building efforts could pay big dividends. How big? Consider this ad from the back of a drugstore trade magazine: "For sale: Drug store in southwestern Ohio college town. Doing good business. Fountain alone more than pays all expenses including heat, light and rest of residence. Gold mine for Physician-Druggist."[9]

"REEL" NICE MOVIE SUNDAE
"Thirty cents is paid for this dish without a murmur."

2 rounded tablespoons crushed
    pitted cherries

2 small scoops vanilla ice cream

1 heaping tablespoon coarsely chopped
    mixed nuts

1 small scoop chocolate ice cream

1 small scoop strawberry ice cream

whipped cream for topping

maraschino cherry for garnish

Layer ingredients in a tall sundae glass in this order: 1 tablespoon cherries topped by 1 scoop vanilla, then the dry nuts. Next the rest of the cherries and the second scoop of vanilla. Then the chocolate and strawberry ice creams, topped with whipped cream and the whole cherry.

SUNDAES

THE FIRST ICE CREAM SUNDAE

"J. B. Porter was there at the invention of the Ice Cream Sundae. Back in 1896 or '97 Porter was the manager at Kaercher's Pharmacy at the corner of Fifth Avenue and Neville Street in Pittsburgh, Pennsylvania. The store's fountain was a popular hang out for high school students from the Shady Side Academy where they would come to get all manner of ice cream sodas and fizzy drinks. However the so-called 'Sunday Blue Laws' which restricted sales of all kinds on Sunday, prevented selling of combinations of ice cream and flavored syrups made with carbonated water.

"No one knows whose idea it was to simply serve the ice cream and flavored syrups without the soda water, but Mr. Porter reported that it had become the custom. On Sunday afternoons, the students would throng into the soda-less fountain and begin shouting out all kinds of combinations as they ordered their 'college ices' to the harassed clerk, George Sunderland, attempting to confuse him, Porter wrote. Sunderland, in repeating the requests back to the ordering students said something along the lines of this being a 'Sunday affair' and asking if they wanted a 'Sunday.' The name stuck. And as these students scattered to 'practically all the larger colleges, the name was carried with them.'

"Porter concluded, 'the popularity of the dish itself [may be] deduced from the fact that more than 2,000 formulas for different kinds of sundaes have already been published and there are probably twice that number which have never seen the light of print.'" —The International Confectioner, March 1921

College Parfait Sundae

This parfait is a layered treat, not a blended one.

¼ cup crushed peeled, pitted peaches
1 small scoop vanilla ice cream
¼ cup crushed strawberries
1 small scoop strawberry ice cream
3 strawberries
whipped cream for topping
maraschino cherry for garnish

In a 12-ounce soda glass, layer the fruit and ice cream in the order given. Fill to the top with whipped cream and garnish with a cherry.

ON THE ROAD

With World War I over and the twenties ready to "roar," people were buy-ing cars and setting out to see the sights. Car registrations tripled from seven million passenger cars to twenty-two million in 1933. And those cars weren't just sitting around the garage or puttering about town: "Owing to the improvement of highways connecting the East and West, North and South, the wide range of utility of the motor car, and the average American's love for the outdoors—adventure—hundreds of thousands of person[s] this year have, with comfort, spent the summer traveling about the United States in automobiles."[1]

As one motor tourist related, the drive across the country involved plenty of stopping in small towns. In 1922 Katherine Lafitte, her sister, and her brother-in-law drove four thousand miles in five weeks. From east to west they camped out in "car parks," cooked their meals over campfires, and met loads of other travelers. As she wrote in an *Outing* magazine article: "Through thirteen states we bowled along, seeing America first . . . And we like the little towns; we drank their ice cream sodas all the way from Boston to Seattle."[2]

Ever-alert soda fountain men saw ways to capture these business oppor-tunities as hundreds of thousands of Americans spent the summer travel-ing the nation's roadways. *Popular Science* reported that in the late teens and early twenties "motor touring increased fifty percent annually." Putting up welcoming billboards "on much traveled highways" on the edge of town was one way to attract travelers to stop at the local soda fountain or drugstore. According to one go-getter, the signs should read "Road Information Free" and "Maps, Blue Books, Hotel Lists at Brown's Drug Store." The unnamed expert advised, "A sign like this large enough so the tourist can not miss it and set so that it can be easily read while going at 30 miles an hour will bring more than enough people to pay for its installation."[3]

Soda and sundae recipes in fountain trade magazines suggested that fountain men capitalize on the travel urge by serving dishes named after top tourist attractions and "aim to feature some of the unusual drinks which are popular in other parts of the country. It is easy to establish a reputation through people who travel."[4]

Yosemite Sundae

1 small scoop each strawberry, vanilla, and chocolate ice cream
2 tablespoons crushed pineapple
2 tablespoons chopped walnuts or pecans
whipped cream for topping

Place the scoops of ice cream in a banana split dish or bowl. Sprinkle with crushed pineapple and nuts and top with whipped cream.

DRINKING AND DRIVING

"It is high time that Prohibition appears upon the scene. In these days of Automobiles it is more necessary than ever that ours should be a Sober Nation. With the greatest of care auto accidents can not be entirely averted: but the whirling dizzy intoxicated brains of auto drivers can not but increase automobile accidents greatly." —Unsigned and undated letter sent to Congressman Andrew Volstead, Minnesota Historical Society collections

El Capitan

1 small scoop each pineapple sherbet, vanilla ice cream, and orange sherbet
2 tablespoons crushed strawberries
2 tablespoons chopped almonds
whipped cream for topping
chocolate almonds for garnish

Arrange the ice cream in a banana split dish. Put the strawberries and then the almonds in between the scoops. Top each scoop with whipped cream and a few chocolate almonds.

Golden Gate Sundae

2 medium scoops strawberry ice cream
2 tablespoons sliced strawberries
2 tablespoons chopped orange sections
whipped cream for topping
strawberries for garnish

Put the ice cream in a banana split dish. Pour the strawberries over one scoop and the oranges over the other. Top with whipped cream and garnish each scoop with a strawberry.

Portland Delight Sundae

1 thin square slice nut pound cake (page 156)
1 large scoop vanilla ice cream
3 tablespoons crushed loganberries, or substitute blueberries
2 tablespoons chopped almonds
1 small scoop orange water ice (Italian ice) or sherbet
maraschino cherry for garnish

Put the pound cake in the middle of a small plate. Top with the vanilla ice cream, flattening slightly with a fork to cover the cake. Pour the berries on top and then the almonds. Center the scoop of orange sherbet on the ice cream and top with a cherry.

HOW MEN ACT WHEN THEY CAN'T GET A DRINK

"Many men are having a little family 'spree' by taking their wives out to dinner. In the old days there used to be a line of men at our telephone booths between five and six in the afternoon calling up their homes to announce that 'business' was going to keep them downtown and not to expect them for dinner. In most of these cases the visit to the telephone booth was followed by a more or less protracted sojourn at the bar and by a dinner, with the trimmings of drinks, in the grill-room. There is still a certain amount of this late afternoon telephoning; but the message now is more often than not an invitation to the man's wife to 'come on down-town and have dinner.'" —E. M. Statler, in *The American Magazine*, June 1919

Raspberry Refresher

"This combination is very pleasing. On a hot day the water ice with the ice cream is preferable to syrup."

1 small scoop vanilla or chocolate ice cream
1 small scoop raspberry ice (Italian ice) or sherbet

Put the ice cream and then the sherbet in a tall sundae glass.

Golden Sunset

"This should sell for 10 or 15 cents."

1 small scoop vanilla ice cream

2 tablespoons crushed orange sections
    or orange marmalade

1 tablespoon finely chopped pitted cherries

whole cherry for garnish

Place the ice cream in a sundae dish, top with oranges and cherries, and garnish with a single pitted cherry.

The soda fountain bubbles with the versatility of American life.

THE INTERNATIONAL CONFECTIONER, APRIL 1919

SODA SHOPS APPEAL TO ALL

"Never has there been such an extraordinary multiplication of shops and counters where . . . hot and cold sodas, bouillons, milk-and-egg drinks, and the like are to be had as within the last six months since the enactment of prohibition. No longer are ice cream sodas and nut sundaes and hot fountain drinks to be regarded as feminine luxuries and dissipations. There are as many men as women customers at these unscreened bars. What the ultimate effect on the national health may be remains to be seen, but so far all that is visible is that one health officer after another is pointing with pride to the lowest death rates on record, and we know well that as a disturber of the stomach alcohol is a champion and sugar a mere amateur." —Practical Druggist and Pharmaceutical Review of Reviews, December 1921

Cubists' Delight

1 slice vanilla ice cream

2 tablespoons crushed red raspberries

2 tablespoons crushed pineapple

whipped cream

2 cubes fresh or canned pineapple

¼ cup fresh or mandarin orange slices

Put the ice cream on a plate. Neatly cover half of it with crushed raspberries and the other half with crushed pineapple. Put a stripe of whipped cream down the middle and top with the cubes of pineapple. Arrange orange slices around the edge of the ice cream.

League of Nations

1 large scoop chocolate ice cream

3 tablespoons Hot Chocolate Fudge Sundae Sauce (page 42)

¼ cup whipped cream, approximately

2 tablespoons chocolate sprinkles

2 tablespoons pecan halves

Put the ice cream in a bowl. Drizzle with chocolate sauce and then cover completely with whipped cream. Sprinkle with chocolate and pecans.

> The increased consumption of ice cream, which
> is generally ascribed to prohibition, has caused
> a scarcity of skilled ice cream makers.
>
> *THE SODA FOUNTAIN, FEBRUARY 1921*

THE FEMALE OF THE SPECIES

When you see the bums and brewers and the riffraff of the land
Out opposing votes for women with a zeal to beat the band
You can mark it down as certain as the signs that never fail
That the female of the species is more deadly than the male!

When the crooked politician begins to froth and foam
And proclaim that women's province is the precinct of the home
'Tis a sign he knows destruction is camping on his trail
And that the female of the species is more deadly than the male!

When the hypocrite sky pilot crawls behind Apostle Paul
And says women should keep silence he has less of sense than gall
For without the goodly women surely Satan would prevail
But the female of the species is more deadly than the male!

When liquor license parties very pointedly and clear
Tell the great white ribbon army to be seated in the rear
It is simple as a primer to a graduate of Yale
That the female of the species is more deadly than the male!

When the grafting legislator, who buys his way with booze,
Votes to keep from womankind her just and legal dues
He has an eye for business—that of keeping out of jail—
For the female of the species is more deadly than the male!

Be men and give her credit due and power to her arm,
And only place within her reach the foe that worketh harm
Then shall the wicked flee away like chaff before the gale
For the female of the species is more deadly than the male!

FRANK E. HERRICK, *PROHIBITION POEMS AND OTHER VERSE*, 1914

A Suffragist

1 banana

3 Thin Walnut Wafers (pages 154–55)

3 small scoops ice cream, any
flavor you prefer

3 tablespoons crushed pineapple

3 strawberries

whipped cream or marshmallow crème

Peel the banana and slice in half lengthwise; place in a banana split dish.
Put the three wafer cookies across the banana. Put a scoop of ice cream on
each wafer. Top each ice cream mound with pineapple and a strawberry. Put
whipped cream or marshmallow crème in between the scoops of ice cream.

If it is necessary to attach such long hard
names to fountain products why not give
them a name that has some suggestion, at
least, of the nature of the thing.

*PRACTICAL DRUGGIST AND PHARMACEUTICAL
REVIEW OF REVIEWS, MAY 1921*

VARIED AND ARTISTIC SUNDAES

"Sundaes and desserts unquestionably offer the greatest opportunity for the artistic and ambitious dispenser to exercise his ingenuity in the preparation of attractive delicacies. An appeal should be made to the eye as well as to the taste. The use of bananas, oranges, cantaloupes, candied fruits, and pastries offer constructive material." —Practical Druggist and Pharmaceutical Review of Reviews, November 1921

Cantaloupe Boat

¼ cantaloupe, cut as a wedge
1 small scoop vanilla ice cream
1 small scoop orange sherbet
2 tablespoons orange syrup
whipped cream for topping

Put the cantaloupe quarter upright on a plate. Carefully place the scoops of ice cream and sherbet in the cantaloupe "boat," scooping out a bit of a hollow if necessary to get them to balance. Drizzle with orange syrup and top with whipped cream.

> There was a dear girl of Lamountain
> Who got her a job at a fountain
> Her smile was so sweet
> On the patrons she'd meet
> The profits went up beyond countin'
>
> *THE SODA FOUNTAIN, JANUARY 1921*

Cherry Royal

"This sundae will make a hit with your male patrons, as it is not too rich, and most men like cherries. Advertise the sundae by signs in the window or at the fountain and charge 20 or 25 cents."

1 large scoop vanilla ice cream
12 large black cherries, pitted
3 tablespoons Cherry Royal Sauce (page 43)
whipped cream for topping
red and green maraschino cherries for garnish

Put the scoop of ice cream in the center of a small plate. Arrange the black cherries around the edge of the ice cream. Pour the cherry sauce over the ice cream, and top with whipped cream and the maraschino cherries.

There is growing up a generation that never saw a saloon and no more thinks it necessary to greet a friend with a drink than to throw in a sandwich with every introduction.
WILLIS J. ABBOT "PROHIBITION IN PRACTICE," *COLLIER'S*, MAY 17, 1919

MEN LOSE SALOONS AS SOCIAL CLUBS

"There were thousands of saloons which were in a measure public clubrooms where men would sit for hours over a glass of beer and talk things over. The ice-cream soda and candy store does not take the place of these saloons, for where there are ladies constantly coming and going, buying candy or ice cream or where there are girl waitresses, a man does not feel at ease to lounge and linger as he did in the old-time public clubrooms." —I. C. Jonas, *Printer's Ink,* August 5, 1920

Just Right Sundae

1 medium scoop vanilla ice cream
1 peach, peeled and sliced
12 blackberries, approximately
3 tablespoons Hot Chocolate Fudge Sundae Sauce (page 42)
marshmallow crème for topping

Put the ice cream in the center of a small plate. Gently press the peach slices into the side of the ice cream. Surround it with the blackberries, drizzle with chocolate sauce, and top with a dab of marshmallow crème.

Southern Special

1 medium scoop vanilla ice cream

1 ounce (2 tablespoons) ginger syrup

2 tablespoons chopped pecans

Put the ice cream in a bowl or sundae dish. Drizzle with syrup and top with pecans.

Cherry Blossom

1 thin slice plain pound cake (page 156)

1 medium scoop Tutti Frutti ice cream (page 31)

3 tablespoons crushed pitted cherries

marshmallow crème for topping

maraschino cherry for garnish

Put the cake on a small plate. Top with ice cream, crushed cherries, and then a dab of marshmallow crème. Garnish with the cherry.

TOUGH PROHIBITION ENFORCER TALKS

Marshall Cox of Tampa, the toughest booze chaser of all. I told him I had come to talk to him about Prohibition. He heaved a giant sigh.

"Young fellow," he said, "I'm all in. What with rambling around these swamps and killin' moonshiners and getting' shot at and bein' bit by mosquitoes, I've got the shakin' fever and I jes' can't go out today. I know where I can get a schooner full o' liquor this minute. But I ain't got the men and I'm a—shakin' so, I jes' can't shoot."

"But just 'cause you catch me sick I'm goin' to take you in my flivver down to see the fleet I ketched."

He took me down the street, put me in a rattly old car that shook as much as he did, and drove me down to the river. There he had eight schooners and launches which he had commandeered. —"Who's Drinking in America," *Cosmopolitan,* December 1921

Grapefruit Sundae

1 pink or red grapefruit
sugar, to taste
1 medium scoop vanilla ice cream
maraschino cherry for garnish

Cut the grapefruit in half. Using a small serrated knife, cut around the edge of each exposed section and sprinkle each half with a tablespoon of sugar. Let stand until the sugar is dissolved, then gently squeeze the sections and the accumulated juices into a shallow bowl. Sprinkle another 2 tablespoons of sugar over the grapefruit. Stir until it is dissolved. Taste and add more sugar as necessary. Serve over vanilla ice cream and garnish with a cherry.

California

¼ cup orange marmalade
¼ cup orange syrup
1 large scoop vanilla ice cream
whipped cream for topping
maraschino cherry for garnish

Stir the marmalade and syrup together. Pour over ice cream. Top with whipped cream and cherry.

ICE MEN REPORT THAT HOME BREW GROWS

One member stated that the home brew by the families in his territory was taking the place of the saloons; he said there was one family that come to the plant five times on a Sunday to get a ten-cent piece of ice to put in their still. He said he considered that a good customer. He said that in his locality there were many families that distill on Sundays. They start on Saturday night and work until Monday morning.

"THE EFFECT OF PROHIBITION ON THE ICE BUSINESS,"
ICE AND REFRIGERATION, DECEMBER 1920

MINNEAPOLIS TRADE BOOMS

"Can ice cream and soda take the place of alcoholic beverages?

"Ice cream and soft drink manufacturers of Minneapolis think that they can. And they back up their opinions with the figures of their sales since July 1 which show an increase of more than 50 per cent, over the month of July last year.

"Local soft drink dealers declare that there is a greater demand for pop and soda than for 'near' beer and other substitutes for alcoholic beverages . . . While police records say nothing of the increase in ice cream soda and soda pop sales, they show that the number of prisoners in the workhouse during the month of July was but one-half of the number for July 1918, while other figures show a similar drop."—The International Confectioner, October 1919

Peach Melba Sundae

2 small scoops vanilla ice cream

1 small scoop lemon sherbet

1½ ounces (3 tablespoons) peach syrup

3 teaspoons roasted slivered almonds

whipped cream for topping

Alternate the scoops of ice cream and sherbet in a banana split dish. Top with the peach syrup, almonds, and a bit of whipped cream.

Peach Fromage

½ peeled fresh or canned peach
1 small scoop maple ice cream
whipped cream for topping
1 tablespoon chopped almonds

Put the peach half cut side-up in a small flat bowl, such as a sherbet dish. Put the maple ice cream in the peach hollow. Top with whipped cream and sprinkle with the almonds.

CREATING APPEALING FOUNTAIN SPECIALS

A "Fountain Specialty" list is an economy. Very often fresh fruits or other dainties are left over from the day before. The quantity is so small yet you dislike to discard it, for it is in merchandisable condition. A few peaches may be left over from fresh peach sundaes featured the day before. Combine a few slices with whipped cream and chocolate ice cream, serve in a parfait glass and call it a fresh peach puff . . . Make use of your leftovers in . . . "fountain specials."

NORTHWEST DRUGGIST, OCTOBER 1922

STOCKPILING ALCOHOLIC BEVERAGES LEGALLY

"The days before Prohibition when everybody who had any money or was supposed to have any money laid in supplies of alcoholic drinks. It became the thing to have a cellar. The larger the cellar, the larger one's pocketbook seemed to be. No man who was anybody in a community dared to say that he was not filling his cellar. It was a legal thing to do; a great drought was in sight; the hospitality of future days depended upon filling the cellar there and then. And so American cellars in apartment houses and hotel rooms and elsewhere were supposedly filled to the kitchen floor. Time has emptied those cellars . . . But hospitality could not be abated. The cellar must seem full, even if it isn't. And so the family bootlegger has come into his own." —"Who's Drinking in America?" *Cosmopolitan,* December 1921

Pear Parfait

½ peeled and cored fresh or canned pear
1 small scoop chocolate ice cream
1 ounce (2 tablespoons) orange syrup
whipped cream for topping
1 tablespoon diced crystallized ginger

Slice the pear half in quarters and carefully arrange them along the sides of a sundae glass. Drop in the scoop of chocolate ice cream and drizzle with the orange syrup. Top with whipped cream and sprinkle with the candied ginger.

Grape Pineapple Sherbet

1 small scoop pineapple sherbet
1 ounce (2 tablespoons) grape juice
maraschino cherry for garnish

Put the sherbet in a small dish. Drizzle with grape juice and decorate with the cherry.

 Ed: How did he manage to sell that old, haunted house?
Co-ed: He started a rumor that there were spirits in the cellar.

CONGRESSMAN LAGUARDIA MAKES BEER AT A SODA FOUNTAIN

"LaGuardia produces real beer by mixing two legal beverages sold at practically all soda fountains. One-third 'near beer' was mixed with two-thirds malt extract. This extract, which is labeled 'for medicinal purposes' has a three per cent alcoholic content, which with the one-half per cent of the near beer, gave the finished product an alcoholic content of 2.17 per cent.

"Representative LaGuardia, who had advertised the demonstration as a test of prohibition, had movies taken of himself standing on the corner and mixing a drink for Charles Ross, truck driver for the J. M. Horton Ice Cream Company, who pulled his horses to a stop when he saw the beer mixing. Ross proved a likely movie student in 'registering delight' and smacking his lips after a long swallow.

"The test fell down as far as Representative LaGuardia's efforts to have himself arrested were concerned. Patrolman John Mennella, on the beat, pushed his way through the crowd supposing an accident had occurred.

"'I'm making beer,' LaGuardia announced when the policeman confronted him.

"'All right,' said Mennella.

"'Why don't you arrest me?'

"'I guess that's a job for a prohibition agent if anyone.'

"'Well, I'm defying you. I thought you might accommodate me.'

"But Mennella couldn't see it that way . . .

"The Congressman was on the scene promptly at 9 o'clock in the morning . . . As reporters and cameramen began to gather Murray Dubner, soda fountain clerk in the drug store, opened bottles of the extract and near beer. LaGuardia passed glasses to everyone within reach.

"'I've tasted worse—likewise better,' was the general comment of those who drank. More than a dozen bottles of each ingredient were used by the Congressman in standing treat. At prohibition headquarters, Major Chester P. Milles,

administrator, said that he had taken no cognizance of LaGuardia's notice and explained that he had little fear the beverage would become popular because nausea would be induced so much sooner than intoxication.

"J. L. Weinberg, owner of the [malt extract] distributing corporation said that he had requested Representative LaGuardia not to make his demonstration . . . 'Just on account of this stunt, we do not want a single new customer now,' he said. 'We are afraid of new business.'" —"LaGuardia Brews; Policemen Amiable," *New York Times,* July 18, 1928

Independence Day Sundae

1 large scoop vanilla ice cream
1 ounce (2 tablespoons) grape syrup
1 ounce (2 tablespoons) pineapple syrup
1 ounce (2 tablespoons) mint syrup
¼ cup crushed pitted cherries
green maraschino cherry for garnish

Push the ice cream down into an 8-ounce tulip sundae glass. With a pointed soda spoon carve out three channels in the ice cream. Put each of the syrups in one of the channels. Fill to the top with crushed cherries and top with the green cherry.

ICE CREAM KEEPS THE PEACE IN MARYLAND

"G. W. Crabbe, Superintendent, Maryland Anti-Saloon League, reported that Prohibition is making its friends everywhere. Men who were skeptical now tell of the large number of men formerly opposed to Prohibition who admit that it has been a good thing in their own lives. Where men are continually together will be found exhibits which prove that Prohibition is a success. There has been a strike among the shipmen in the city, but with little disturbance. This is largely due to the fact that the men do not have the open saloon and that they have substituted the ice cream cone for the beer mug." —Ernest Hurst Cherrington, editor, *Anti-Saloon League Yearbook,* 1920

Salamander

1 ounce (2 tablespoons) ginger syrup, or substitute vanilla syrup
1 teaspoon minced crystallized ginger
1 small scoop vanilla ice cream
dash ground cinnamon for garnish
maraschino cherry for garnish

Combine the ginger syrup with the crystallized ginger. Put the ice cream in a small dish and pour syrup over top. Dust with cinnamon and top with cherry.

Creamed Fig

"On account of the popularity of figs and the great number of people who eat figs for so many purposes, this formula is a trade winner. Charge 15 cents."

2 tablespoons fig jam

1 small scoop chocolate ice cream, or substitute 1 small scoop vanilla ice
   cream topped with 2 tablespoons chocolate syrup

whipped cream for topping

maraschino cherry for garnish

2 Thin Walnut Wafers (pages 154–55)

Stir the jam, adding a few drops of water, if necessary, to make it into a topping consistency. Put the ice cream in a sundae dish. Top with the fig topping and whipped cream. Garnish with the cherry and serve wafers on the side.

"The newspaper cartoonists will have to change their style once prohibition comes in. They'll only be able to do dry humor."

HOTEL BAR CHANGES BRING BETTER CUSTOMERS

"All over the country big hotels are about ready to change the old bar-rooms to up-to-date soda and ice cream parlors. Those hotels that have had such peaceful adjuncts running any length of time have found a profit in it and a larger luncheon and afternoon tea trade. While the profits have not equaled the old bar, the change in the class of people visiting the hotel has been for the better."
—"Changing Conditions," *The International Confectioner,* June 1919

Black-eyed Daisy

1 (⅛-inch thick) slice Neapolitan ice cream
7 almond halves
1 raisin

Place the slice of ice cream on a small plate. Arrange the almonds in the center like the petals of a daisy with the raisin as the center.

Tourist Special

Perfect for a backyard picnic. A sundae in hand with no dishes to wash.

1 cup-style ice cream cone
1 medium scoop vanilla ice cream, softened
½ ounce (1 tablespoon) chocolate syrup
1 tablespoon chopped pecans

Fill ice cream cone nearly full with soft vanilla ice cream, gently pushing it well down into the cone. Make a well in the center with a spoon and add the chocolate syrup. Top with chopped pecans and serve with a spoon.

The Tasty Toasty

D. J. Fitzgerald sent this sundae idea to *Soda Fountain* magazine: "The author states that he realizes the fact that but few 5-cent dishes are offered at the soda fountain for the public, and he therefore submits this formula for a 5-cent specialty which has proved a big winner for him."

1 medium scoop vanilla ice cream
1 ounce (2 tablespoons) real maple syrup
¼ cup corn flake cereal

Put the ice cream in a dish. Drizzle with maple syrup and a sprinkling of corn flakes.

LOVE AT THE SODA SHOP

"The soda fountain often plays an important part in fanning the flame of love . . . Many fountain owners are finding there is a great demand for drinks with names like kiss me again, some day, soul kiss, lover's delight [. . .] what better could quicken a bashful lover than to have his coy companion say I would like a soul kiss wouldn't you, John?" —The Soda Fountain, December 1921

Cupid Delight Sundae

1 (⅛-inch) slice vanilla ice cream

3 tablespoons crushed pineapple

3 cubes canned or fresh pineapple

4 maraschino cherries

3 tablespoons crushed strawberries

2 Thin Walnut Wafers (pages 154–55)

Cut the ice cream in half across the long edge and place the two slices side by side on a plate. Pour the crushed pineapple over one slice and top with the pineapple cubes arranged in a circle with 1 cherry in the center. Pour the strawberries over the other ice cream slice and arrange the remaining 3 cherries in a circle on top of it. Put the wafers on the side and serve with two spoons.

Cupid Delight—Another Version

1 small scoop caramel ice cream

2 tablespoons chopped fresh
   or canned apricots

1 tablespoon chopped almonds

whipped cream for topping

whole almond for garnish

Serve the ice cream in a small dish topped with the apricots and chopped almonds. Garnish with whipped cream and the whole almond.

Cupid's Garden

1 large scoop vanilla ice cream

1½ ounces (3 tablespoons) strawberry syrup

1 tablespoon cinnamon heart-shaped candies

Put the ice cream in a sundae dish and pour the syrup over the top. Sprinkle with the cinnamon candies.

Have-a-Date Sundae

1 large scoop maple nut ice cream

1 ounce (2 tablespoons) Hot Chocolate Fudge Sundae Sauce (page 42)

2 tablespoons shredded coconut

whipped cream for topping

walnut-stuffed date for garnish

Put the ice cream in a sundae dish. Drizzle with the chocolate sauce and sprinkle with coconut. Top with whipped cream and garnish with the stuffed date.

> In the spring a young man's fancy lightly turns to thoughts of love, while the young woman's fancy yearningly turns to ice cream sodas. Better cater to her fancy.
>
> *THE SODA FOUNTAIN, MARCH 1921*

BOOTLEGGERS ADJUSTING WELL

"Bootleggers are the only people in America who have adjusted themselves completely to prohibition. Providing America with alcoholic drink is now a well-organized business with an income estimated at over three billion dollars a year.

"In 1929 prohibition authorities raided nearly sixteen thousand distilleries and seized over eleven thousand stills many of them giant affairs two or three stories tall." —E. E. Free, "Where America Gets Its Booze," *Popular Science,* May 1930

St. Patrick's Special

2 small scoops mint sherbet or ice cream

1 small scoop vanilla ice cream

1 ounce (2 tablespoons) chocolate syrup

1 mint gumdrop for garnish

Put a scoop of mint sherbet or ice cream in the bottom of a sundae glass. Top with the vanilla ice cream and chocolate syrup. Then put the second scoop of mint on top and garnish with the gumdrop.

Yellow Chick Sundae

1 large scoop strawberry ice cream
1 large scoop vanilla ice cream
2 tablespoons marshmallow crème
few drops yellow food coloring
¼ cup shredded coconut
2 tablespoons chopped black walnuts
12 large jellybeans or other candy eggs
small plastic or paper chick on a pick for garnish

Put the strawberry ice cream and then the vanilla ice cream in a tall, tulip-shaped sundae dish. Stir together marshmallow crème and food coloring, and top ice cream with yellow marshmallow crème. Sprinkle the top with coconut and black walnuts. Arrange the jellybeans or candy eggs around the edge of the dish and decorate with the plastic chick.

Easter Strawberry

"Some sweet Sunday. Only 20 cents. Mighty Fine!"

3 tablespoons crushed strawberries
1 large scoop vanilla ice cream
3 tablespoons Royal Easter Dressing (recipe follows)
whipped cream for topping

Put the crushed strawberries in the bottom of a sundae glass. Add the ice cream and top with the Royal Easter Dressing. Garnish with whipped cream.

Royal Easter Dressing

⅓ cup honey
¼ cup sweet cream
½ cup marshmallow crème
few drops purple food coloring

Carefully stir the honey and cream together. Fold this mixture into the marshmallow crème and then add the food coloring a drop at a time. Use immediately.

Prohibition will be enforced if we stick to it long enough. Ten years is but a little time with 100,000 years ahead.

CARRIE CHAPMAN CATT, 1930

Walnut Sandwich

1 (½-inch) slice vanilla ice cream
¼ cup chopped walnuts, plus 1 tablespoon for garnish
2 tablespoons butterscotch sauce

Cut the sliced ice cream in half to mimic two slices of bread and put one slice on a small plate. Sprinkle the ¼ cup walnuts on the ice cream and top with the second slice. Spoon the butterscotch on top and garnish with remaining walnuts.

Almond Sally

1 large scoop maple ice cream
1 ounce (2 tablespoons) chocolate syrup
5 almonds
1 tablespoon chopped dates
whipped cream for garnish

Put the ice cream in a shallow dish or bowl. Cover with chocolate syrup. Arrange the almonds in a star shape on top of the ice cream and sprinkle with the chopped dates. Put the whipped cream around the edges.

> Americans don't stay dry. At home they are in favor of Prohibition; when they go a-visiting, it is often another matter . . . While Florida does not boast of this fact—that it will be wet this winter—Florida doesn't care what prospective tourists know it.
>
> "WHO'S DRINKING IN AMERICA," *COSMOPOLITAN*, DECEMBER 1921

TOP ENFORCEMENT OFFICIAL SHARES INSIDE PROHIBITION VIEWS

Mabel W. Willebrandt, Former Assistant United States Attorney General in Charge of Prohibition Cases from 1921 to 1929 wrote of her experiences and shared her opinions.

"Politics and liquor apparently are as inseparable a combination as beer and pretzels. You can neither coax, scold, nor nag the people into law observance. Consequently enforcement is the necessary approach at this time . . .

"We cannot forget that as long as a large number of people have a thirst for alcoholic stimulants and other people have a desire to 'make big money quick' liquor will be produced and consumed, in spite of laws or officers of the law.

"A simple calculation shows how much money can be made in these transactions . . . One carload of pure alcohol would make 64,000 quarts of synthetic whiskey. At $4 a quart the ten cars reached a bootleg value of $2,560,000. Even if obliged to bribe a few city police and deduct the price of bottling and delivery, the conspirators made a small fortune on an initial outlay in the form of a bribe of only $6,000 . . .

"Before I lived so close to repulsive facts of this kind, I found it possible to be much more unconcerned at the sight of really splendid people of high principles imbibing bootleg liquors. Repeatedly facing the trail of bribery and ugly, unfair profits in the hands of racketeers, which every quart of whiskey signals today, I cannot put aside the conviction that the price is too high . . .

"Truly, the ingenuity of those who crave a drink is only exceeded by that of those who are willing to supply the wherewithal to satisfy the craving . . .

"The Eighteenth Amendment is not nearly so much a victory as it is a challenge.

"The predominating dry sentiment among the women of the country is not noticeable, of course, among those who congregate in country clubs and those who have plenty of leisure and very little work. I am well aware, also, that more of the girls and women who are employed in offices and industry are drinking now than was the case ten years ago. Nevertheless, anyone who mingles freely with all classes of women is bound to discover very soon that the majority are opposed utterly and unalterably to reestablishment of open saloons and they think any *relaxation of enforcement is a step in that direction. The great majority of women still lean economically upon men, their fathers or their husbands . . .*

"*The saloons not only deprived women of the companionship to which they thought they were entitled, but saloons absorbed money which the women felt they were entitled to share. For selfish reasons, quite as much as moral reasons, the women of the country will continue to be strongly for prohibition.*" —Mabel Walker Willebrandt, *The Inside of Prohibition*

Moonbeams

1 large scoop vanilla ice cream

3 tablespoons marshmallow crème

2 tablespoons shredded coconut

1 tablespoon chopped walnuts

whipped cream for garnish

Layer the ingredients in a tall sundae glass in the order given.

POPULARITY OF CHOCOLATE

"In days gone by the favorite flavor at the soda fountain was strawberry, but now the trend of public taste has turned to chocolate. Twenty gallons of chocolate syrup are used to every gallon of other flavoring . . . Its food value, too, is considerably more than that of the fruit flavors and combined with the malted milk almost makes a luncheon." —Practical Druggist and Pharmaceutical Review of Reviews, July 1921

Chocolate Temptation

1 small scoop chocolate ice cream

1 ounce (2 tablespoons) dark chocolate syrup

2 tablespoons chopped roasted almonds

2 tablespoons marshmallow crème

1 blanched almond for garnish

Put the chocolate ice cream in a small sundae glass. Cover with the chocolate syrup, chopped almonds, and marshmallow crème. Garnish with the single almond.

Sultana Sundae

1 medium scoop maple ice cream

1 ounce (2 tablespoons) chocolate syrup

2 tablespoons chopped raisins

2 tablespoons chopped pecans

Put the ice cream in a small sundae glass. Spoon the chocolate syrup over the top and sprinkle with the raisins and pecans.

Soldier Boy Kiss

1 small scoop chocolate ice cream

2 tablespoons butterscotch syrup

Put the ice cream in a small dish and cover with butterscotch.

A former saloon keeper in a southern city says that his receipts run almost as high as they did when liquors and beer were sold and his license money now goes to pay the rent. He figures that he is breaking about even.

THE INTERNATIONAL CONFECTIONER, MAY 1919

No Free Lunch

"You had to have the nickel [for a tub of beer]
before you could get the free lunch for nothing."

"Knocked for a Goal," *The Textile Worker*

BY THE TIME THE STATES RATIFIED Prohibition in 1919, the glory days of the saloon-provided free lunch were gone. Its decline started with patriotic participation in voluntary World War I food conservation efforts. In July 1917, just three months after the United States entered the war, William McClenhan, president of the five thousand–member New York City Retail Liquor Dealers Association, analyzed the cost and amount of food savings that would go to the war effort as the group voted to eliminate free lunches: "There are about 3,000 places giving free lunches. That means, in the aggregate, that between $20,000 and $25,000 a day can be saved in food because the average free lunch counter costs about $6 to $8 a day."[1]

During its heyday, the quality of free lunches varied greatly. In 1901 a temperance group, "The Committee of Fifty," commissioned an investigation on saloon conditions. They reported that in eastern cities—Boston, New York, Baltimore, and Philadelphia—a cold lunch of bread, crackers, wafers, cheese, bologna sausage, weinerwurst, cold eggs, sliced tomatoes, cold meats, salads, pickles, and other rel-

ishes was the usual fare. Patrons' favorites were pickles, salt meats, sauerkraut, and potato salad. Some places served a hot lunch of soup and bread and occasionally a noontime roasted meat with some vegetables and a relish. Even then, New Orleans was a gastronomic step above the rest. Saloons there typically offered two tables of free food: one with bread, butter, salad, and sauces, and the other with a large tureen of soup, a platter of roast beef, and a large dish of rice or baked beans or hash or mashed potatoes. While the report did not provide menus for the western parts of the country, it indicated that the "free lunch is more elaborate in Chicago, St. Louis, and San Francisco." One Chicago establishment served 150 to 200 pounds of meat, 1.5 to 2 bushes of potatoes, 50 loaves of bread, 35 pounds of beans, 45 dozen eggs, 10 dozen ears of corn, and $1.50 to $2.00 in vegetables daily, costing thirty to forty dollars a day.[2]

The New York Retail Liquor Dealers Association's actions were ahead of much of the country. Herbert Hoover would not officially be named wartime food administrator until August 1917, and in October he would call for hotel and restaurant food restrictions. As association head McClenhan explained the vote at a secret meeting in July 1917: "There was considerable opposition to the resolution abolishing this phase of our business, but they all joined and made it unanimous when it was pointed out that we owe something to the efforts made in the direction of food conservation." After the war, economic conditions and Prohibition's handwriting on the wall kept the lunch counters empty. Still, the memory of laden tables and lightly arrayed bars fueled myths of hospitality.[3]

The decline of saloons' free lunches opened the door for soda fountains' luncheonettes. Even in wet states, pre-Prohibition soda fountains attracted new customers now that everyone had to pay for lunch. And, as one of the trade journals reported in 1920, the luncheonette business paved the way for acceptance of Prohibition: "Less than five years ago the conventional lunch of the busy man was a ham sandwich and a glass of beer, or if he patronized a pick up restaurant a ham sandwich and a cup of coffee. Today this has been generally replaced by the sandwich and the malted chocolate or similar drink. The fight which the soda fountain has been waging for temperance has prepared the way, and a large proportion of regular drinkers will now follow the well-beaten path to the soda fountain or 'Coffee Room.'"[4]

For laboring men, the question of replacing the saloon was far more material than where to eat lunch: "The saloon was to the working man what the City

Bars in small towns were just as much a social center for a man's refreshment as big-city saloons. Before World War I food conservation efforts, the counter was lined with "free lunch" options.

Club, the Union League Club, the University Club and similar organizations are to hundreds of other men. The spirit of democracy prevailed in the saloon. A five-cent piece placed upon the edge of the bar put a man upon an equality with every other man in the place."[5]

Indeed, John Collier, president of the National Community Centre Association, explained that the saloons "are the social centres, loafing places, places where things are talked over under conditions of freedom, where the heavy weight of life is for a brief time lifted from the shoulders of workingmen ... where good-fellowship and an optimistic frame of mind are the things expected of them."[6]

Additionally, the saloon offered working men and their leaders a free place to meet. As the drums of temperance beat louder, some labor activists attributed union-busting sentiments to the movement: "Prohibition originated in the fertile brain of the Dollar Baron, he did not care the snap of his finger what his employees ate or drank until he discovered that the beverage depot—the saloon—provided a meeting place for the workers, a place where they could exchange views and quite frequently get together, organize and try to secure some of the things which were long being denied to them."[7]

In February 1917, before the United States entered World War I and before Congress took up the concept of prohibition legislation, Samuel Gompers, founder and president of the American Federation of Labor, wrote a letter explaining his belief that labor unions were more effective than prohibition laws would be in bringing about sobriety: "There is no agency so potent to make men temperate in all their habits as the much misunderstood and misrepresented organized labor movement—a movement that brings improvement in the mental and physical stature of our people and reduces to a minimum the desire, the taste, of the habit of intemperance." His position did not sway the states from ratification.[8]

After the Eighteenth Amendment became law, Congress considered the enforcement legislation required to prohibit the "manufacture, sale or transportation of intoxicating liquors." Gompers brought a resolution, passed overwhelmingly at an AF of L meeting representing three million members, calling for continuation of low (2¾ percent alcohol) beer permitted during the war. Gompers's argument was that this beer was "not intoxicating" and so should be permitted. He testified eloquently to the importance of beer in working men's lives: "I know what a glass of beer meant to me in the midday in the factory full of dust, full of foul air." He described how men digging trenches pooled their money, contributing two or three cents at lunchtime to buy a shared quart or pint of beer. How for factory men "beer is brought in and the men drink it with their well dried out lunch ... Take the man who works in any industrial establishment for eight or nine hours or more a day; how welcome a glass of beer is to him can not be known except to those who have had the industrial experience."[9]

Strict prohibitionists carried the day with only "near beer," at one-half percent alcohol, and nonalcoholic malt beverages allowed to legally substitute for the common mealtime beer. Still, as Gompers testified, "The fact is that you do not cure the evils of alcoholism by such legislation so long as people can go into their kitchens and with almost any kind of food or any fruit make some alcohol . . . for themselves."[10]

After drawing the line at alcoholic content, temperance activists sought to support substitutes for the saloon itself. Church women raised money to establish coffeehouses in locations that once were bars. Still, halfway through Prohibition, Rev. Dr. Gustav Arnold Carstensen, rector of New York's Holy Rood Church, said no suitable substitute for the saloon had been furnished. Arthur Davis, state superintendent of New York's Anti-Saloon League, disagreed, declaring that times had changed and citing an "increase in public libraries, the community centres which are spreading in towns and villages, the Y.M.C.A.'s, Y.W.C.A.'s, the Knights of Columbus halls, the great municipally owned recreation centres. Liquor-inspired pastimes are dying and clean sports are coming into their own."[11]

As Prohibition drew to a close, longing for old ways and hopes for the return of saloons grew. One minister who had helped establish a "labor temple" wrote to the editor of the *New York Times:* "With many working men there is still a strong feeling for the 'saloon' which in the old days was the place where they could 'shake out their hearts.'" However, the old-fashioned saloon was not to be. As

liquor sales resumed across the nation, they were under local control. Cities granted operating licenses to bars and restaurants. Free food and free meeting places granted in exchange for alcohol were, indeed, things of the past. The Anti-Saloon League managed a lasting victory over the brewery-owned saloons that had been seen to cause so much social disruption.[12]

RICH BEEF SOUP

2 quarts rich, low-sodium beef stock

1 cup diced cooked beef

¼ cup diced turnip

¼ cup diced rutabaga

¼ cup diced carrot

¼ cup diced onion

1 clove garlic, minced

1 small bay leaf

½ teaspoon ground cloves

1 teaspoon salt, or less to taste

1½ teaspoons pepper

2 heaping tablespoons flour

Set aside ½ cup of the soup stock. Combine all the ingredients except the flour and reserved stock in a 4-quart saucepan. Simmer for about a half hour, or until the vegetables are just tender. Blend the reserved ½ cup stock gradually with the flour, making a smooth paste. Stir into the simmering soup and continue cooking until the soup is slightly thickened. Makes about 4 (2-cup) servings.

FROM THE LUNCHEONETTE

THE FIRST LUNCHEONETTE

"The luncheonette business . . . had its inception in the Twin Cities in 1909. It grew out of the hot chocolate and beef tea trade, developed through the serving of sandwiches, pies and milk into the regular preparation of hot foods and the establishment of menus varying with each day of the week . . . In St. Paul, Neff & Rosenquist, at that time location as at present, Seventh and Jackson streets, was the first firm to go into the luncheonette business.

"C. H. McCoy, who with his Partner Charles McCall, conducted a store at Fourth Street and Second Avenue south, Minneapolis—later sold to the Public Drug Co., is credited with the establishment of the first luncheonette in a drug store in Minneapolis. This was in 1909. Sandwiches, chicken pie, mashed potatoes and salads were served." —Northwest Druggist, March 1922

A FEW NEW SANDWICHES SERVED AT THE CLARIDGE SHOP IN NEW YORK CITY

Currant and Almond

4 ounces (1 cup) toasted almonds, ground or finely chopped
¼ cup currant jelly, or more to make smooth paste

Combine chopped almonds with the currant jelly and spread thinly between slices of graham or whole wheat bread.

Ham and Egg

8 ounces ham, ground or very finely chopped
1 hardboiled egg, very finely chopped
1 teaspoon minced onion
¼ cup mayonnaise
1 teaspoon grated horseradish, to taste

Combine all the ingredients and spread thinly on whole wheat bread.

Ham and Jelly

¼ cup currant jelly, to taste
8 ounces ham, ground or very finely chopped

Gradually combine the jelly with the ham until the mixture is a spreadable consistency. Put between slices of good-quality white bread.

ELEGY ON FREE LUNCH

They have killed Free Lunch, the lovely.
They have gypped Free Lunch the blest,
And the cheese has ceased from troubling
And the pretzels are at rest:
Never more the fork upstanding
From the glass shall glimmer far
As a bright and cheery beacon
To the wanderer at the bar.

Nevermore the wistful onion,
Shall entice the roving eye.
Or the ripe and luscious olive
Lure the weary passerby,
And the sandwich fraught with gravy,
Never more the heart will cheer,
Gone the gracious appetizer,
Gone the codicil to beer.

Fare ye well, my old companion,
Eleemosynary lunch,
Never more I'll share your treasures
With the old-time, hungry bunch;
And my heart is sad and heavy
And the tear is in my eye,
I will miss you when I'm hungry
I will miss you when I'm dry.
I will miss your sweet addendum
To the beaker and the birch
I will miss that lovely lagniappe
On its cool, adjacent perch;

Never more you'll cheer and comfort
With your bounty heaping high,
But I never shall forget you
So, goodbye, Free Lunch, goodbye.
The Sweet Dry and Dry

RECIPE NOTE:
ICE CREAM FOR MORE THAN DESSERT

Happy diners could order ice cream as part of a salad or even small entrees at Prohibition-era lunch counters. The description of the Boston Fruit Salad Sundae in the *Spatula*, a journal for soda fountain operators, touted that the combination "should bring 15 cents at least."

English Delight

½ English muffin, toasted
¼ cup crushed strawberries
1 small scoop strawberry ice cream
whipped cream for topping
maraschino cherry for garnish

Put toasted English muffin half on a plate and cover with crushed strawberries. Put the ice cream in the center and garnish with whipped cream and cherry.

When any saloonkeeper decides to put in a lunch room he will make no gamble, as naturally his daily customers, especially at the noon hour, will go back to the old places because of habit and old associations and acquaintances. These men will all eat ice cream, for the craving will be for sweets to take the place of liquor.

THE INTERNATIONAL CONFECTIONER, FEBRUARY 1919

Boston Fruit Salad Sundae

"This is another form of serving ice cream that is becoming popular and admits of many various and pleasing combinations which may be dispensed under various names. These salads are served on small platters such as are used in hotels for side dishes or a small plate may be used."

1 leaf crisp lettuce
1 medium scoop vanilla ice cream
1 medium scoop strawberry ice cream
2 tablespoons crushed pitted cherries
2 tablespoons crushed pineapple
2 maraschino cherries for garnish

Put the lettuce on a medium salad plate and put the ice creams on either end of the leaf. Pour the crushed cherries over the vanilla ice cream and the pineapple over the strawberry ice cream. Put a cherry on top of each scoop.

Version 2: Use strawberry and chocolate ice creams. Put crushed strawberries on the strawberry and Chop Suey topping (page 48) on the chocolate. Garnish with whipped cream.

Version 3: Use 2 scoops of vanilla ice cream. Top with crushed cherry and crushed pineapple. Crown with a cherry or strawberry and chopped pecans.

> The luncheonette's . . . introduction has been the greatest single development in the industry and has far overshadowed prohibition in its effects on business.
>
> *THE SODA FOUNTAIN, OCTOBER 1921*

RECIPE NOTE:
LIGHT AND SPECIALIZED MEALS

With many soda fountain lunch counters being situated in pharmacies, it made sense that the trade journals would tout the business benefits of offering healthful eating options. Many of the sandwich fillings were combinations of nuts and vegetables. Chicken and ham salads had added greens to lighten them up, and experts suggested that offering meatless lunch options, perhaps with recipes from the meatless days of World War I years earlier, were "an exceedingly good plan."[1]

The *Northwestern Druggist* urged pharmacists who had soda fountain lunch counters to offer rhubarb: "If rhubarb is properly prepared it will be most acceptable in the spring when the system apparently craves the very things rhubarb supplies. Everyone knows rhubarb is among the most healthful of all edible plants and to omit it from the menus because of the complaints of past years is poor business."[2]

Spiced Rhubarb

This sauce can be used as a breakfast dish or as a relish with meats or to add a special flavoring in puddings.

2⅓ pounds rhubarb, coarsely chopped
2 cups sugar, or more to taste
¾ cup vinegar
1 teaspoon cinnamon
¼ teaspoon ground cloves

Combine all the ingredients in a large saucepan. Stir to blend well and then cook over medium heat, stirring until the sugar is fully dissolved. Taste and add more sugar if desired. Lower the heat and cook until the rhubarb breaks down and the sauce is reduced to a smooth marmalade thickness. The sauce will keep in the refrigerator for up to a week and may be frozen.

Nut Loaf

1 cup fresh bread crumbs

1 cup milk

1 cup finely chopped walnuts

1 cup boiled rice

1½ tablespoons melted butter

1 egg, lightly beaten

1 teaspoon salt, or less to taste

¼ teaspoon white pepper

dash cayenne

½ green pepper, chopped

Preheat the oven to 325 degrees. In a medium bowl combine the bread crumbs and milk. Let stand until the milk is mostly absorbed. Add the remaining ingredients and mix well. Press the mixture into a lightly greased loaf pan and bake until set, about 30 to 40 minutes. Serve in slices with or without tomato or horseradish sauce.

SAVINGS FROM PROHIBITION WIDESPREAD

"This committee [of the Brewers Association of America] found that the prosperity which follows prohibition goes first to the savings banks, then to the ice cream and soft drink industry, then to the moving picture and other theaters[,] then to candy, then to tobacco, and then to better general goods." —William H. Shofer, *The International Confectioner,* June 1919

VEGETARIAN MEALS

"Many people will welcome the opportunity of getting a balanced meal, appetizingly served, without the necessity for having to eat meat. For a good, square meal, pick one from each group."

Soups: corn chowder, cereal soup, cream of tomato, celery, asparagus, spinach

Vegetables: baked or boiled sweet or white potatoes, fresh green peas, buttered beets, green corn, sliced cucumbers

Salads: lettuce and tomato salad, vegetable salad, lettuce salad with cheese dressing, pear and cheese salad, alligator pear salad

Main Course: stuffed green peppers, stuffed ripe tomatoes, baked beans in individual casseroles, baked bean cutlets, nut loaf, egg salad, creamed eggs

Bread: corn bread and butter, white bread with peanut butter, white bread sandwiches with orange marmalade filling, bran gems, oatmeal bread

SIMPLE HOT BEVERAGES MAKE WINTER FOUNTAIN SUCCESS

"The fountain need not install an elaborate luncheonette equipment and ser-vice in order to make the winter season a profitable one. Sandwiches, a few hot beverages, cake, doughnuts, and perhaps French pastry are all the food dishes and drinks that are essential." —"Hot Soda," *Midland Druggist and Pharmaceutical Review,* December 1921

Tomato Bisque

Ray Hoote, who owned three fountains in New York City, contributed his rec-ipe for a quickly made tomato bisque to the *Soda Fountain Journal*. This mod-ern adaptation specifies products with low or no sodium.

Bisque Base

1 teaspoon flour

2 tablespoons beef extract (soup base or bouillon)

1 (12-ounce) bottle no-salt Heinz ketchup

1 (14- to 16-ounce) can low-sodium diced tomatoes

salt and pepper to taste

In a medium saucepan, stir the flour and beef extract into the ketchup and then blend in the tomatoes. Cook, stirring frequently over medium heat, until the mixture is slightly thickened. Add salt and pepper to taste. Cool and store in the refrigerator for up to 5 days, or freeze in ice cube trays. Makes enough for 12 servings of Tomato Bisque.

To make single serving:

2 tablespoons Bisque Base

1 teaspoon malted milk powder

2 tablespoons hot water

¾ cup hot milk or water

whipped cream for topping

Combine the Bisque Base with malted milk powder in a mug. Stir in the hot water, and then add hot milk or water to fill. Top with whipped cream.

PRESIDENTIAL LEADERSHIP ESSENTIAL TO PROHIBITION SUCCESS

"Prohibition can be enforced. Not by left-handed efforts. Not by tinkering with the Constitution. Not by wasting time juggling percentages in the Volstead Act. But by intelligent, courageous, systematic, consecrated leadership from the Chief Executive of the nation. You can have such leadership in Herbert Hoover."
—Hoover campaign speech given by Mabel Walker Willebrandt

Chicken Salad

2 cups diced cooked chicken
⅓ cup diced celery
1 hardboiled egg, diced
⅛ cup mayonnaise, or to taste
lettuce leaf for serving

Combine all the ingredients except the lettuce and chill for a half hour. Serve by mounding on a lettuce leaf. Makes about 4 (½-cup) servings.

Ham Salad

1 cup finely chopped cabbage
¼ cup finely chopped onion
1 cup diced celery
½ cup mayonnaise
1 cup diced ham, plus 1 additional cup for serving
lettuce leaf for serving

In a medium mixing bowl, combine the cabbage, onion, celery, and mayonnaise. Stir well and let stand for about 10 minutes. Stir again and add 1 cup diced ham, mixing well. Chill a half hour before serving. Place a piece of lettuce on a salad plate. Mound a half cup of the ham salad in the center and then scatter additional diced ham around the border. Makes about 6 (½-cup) servings.

Cheese and Chicken Salad

½ cup diced chicken
2 hardboiled eggs, diced
¼ cup diced celery
¼ cup finely diced American cheese, or grated Cheddar
⅛ cup mayonnaise, or to taste
lettuce leaf for serving

Combine all the ingredients except the lettuce. Chill for a half hour before serving on lettuce leaf. Makes about 5 (⅓-cup) servings.

Frozen Tomato Salad

1 envelope unflavored gelatin (Knox brand)

¼ cup cold water

1 (28-ounce) can   puree

1 tablespoon corn oil

2 teaspoons vinegar

2 teaspoons freshly squeezed lemon juice

2 teaspoons onion juice

2 teaspoons celery seed

⅛ teaspoon paprika

lettuce leaf for serving

mayonnaise for serving

Sprinkle the gelatin over the cold water, stir, and set aside to soften. In a medium saucepan combine the tomato puree and the remaining ingredients. Bring to a simmer and cook for about 5 minutes. Add the softened gelatin and stir until it is completely dissolved. Put the mixture in the refrigerator to chill and then freeze following the directions of your ice cream maker. To serve, place a small scoop of the frozen salad on a lettuce leaf and top with a dollop of mayonnaise.

HALLOWE'EN IS SPOOKY: TRY CIDER WITH A COOKIE

"Sweet cider has always been very appropriate for Hallowe'en and will be more so this year, for, since prohibition came along, cider has been getting a great deal of attention. A good many people are now talking about it who previously patronized the hard drink emporiums." —Practical Druggist and Pharmaceutical Review, October 1921

Honeysuckle Cakes

4 tablespoons (¼ cup) butter, softened

¾ cup honey

1 egg

½ teaspoon cinnamon

⅛ teaspoon ground cloves

½ teaspoon baking soda

1¾ cups plus 1 tablespoon flour

2 teaspoons water

1 cup very finely chopped raisins

Preheat the oven to 325 degrees. In a large mixing bowl, mix together the butter and honey and then stir in the egg. Add the seasonings and baking soda and 1 cup flour. Stir in the water and then ¾ cup flour. Mix the raisins with the last tablespoon of flour and stir them into the batter. Drop batter by teaspoons onto well-greased baking sheets. Bake until they just turn light brown, about 10 minutes. Makes about 6 dozen small cakes.

Thin Walnut Wafers: Version 1

1 egg, lightly beaten
½ cup sugar
¼ teaspoon baking powder
¼ cup flour
¼ teaspoon salt, optional
4 ounces (1 cup) finely chopped walnuts

NOTE: There isn't any butter in this recipe.

Preheat the oven to 325 degrees. Using an electric mixer, beat the egg and sugar until mixture is light and lemon colored and thickened. Fold in the baking powder, flour, and optional salt. Then fold in the walnuts. Drop by half teaspoons (the equivalent of a measuring teaspoon) on a well-greased baking sheet and smooth with a dampened finger so the batter is about the size of a fifty-cent piece. Bake until just beginning to brown and the top of the cookie looks dry and completely baked, about 5 to 10 minutes. Cool the wafers on the sheet for a minute or two and then carefully remove to a wire rack to finish cooling. Makes about 4 dozen cookies.

Thin Walnut Wafers: Version 2

This version is thinner, crisper, and tastes more like caramel. However, the cookies are more likely to bake faster than you expect. Keep close watch while they're in the oven so they don't burn.

2 eggs
1 cup firmly packed brown sugar
4 ounces (1 cup) very finely chopped walnuts
3 tablespoons flour
¼ teaspoon baking powder

NOTE: There isn't any butter in this recipe.

Preheat the oven to 325 degrees. Using an electric mixer, beat the eggs and brown sugar until thick and light. Stir in the walnuts, flour, and baking powder. Drop by half teaspoons (the equivalent of a measuring teaspoon) onto well-greased baking sheets and smooth with a dampened finger to about the size of a fifty-cent piece. Bake until the edges are just beginning to brown and the top looks dry, about 5 to 10 minutes. Cool the wafers on the sheets for a minute or two and then carefully remove to a wire rack to finish cooling. Makes about 8 dozen cookies.

PROHIBITION AND POLITICS

"You see even if politics and politicians desired to keep out of this business of bootlegging, it is not possible for [them to do so] for the reason that when any man of the sort who goes into bootlegging, whether he is of high station as a boot-legger, or the lowest, gets into trouble his first thought is to secure political influence to get him out. He knows how things work in this country. He knows that it is far more useful for a man who is in the net of the law to have a political pull than it is for him to be innocent." —Samuel G. Blythe, "The Bootleggers," *Saturday Evening Post,* September 23, 1922

Cheap Pound Cake

"Pound cake undoubtedly is the best selling cake at the fountain, and three cakes are usually carried, raisin, plain and nut. Five and ten cent slices are sold."

4 teaspoons baking powder

5 cups flour

12 tablespoons (¾ cup) butter, softened

2 cups sugar

4 large eggs

2 teaspoons lemon extract

1½ cups milk

For nut cake: ¾ cup finely chopped toasted almonds or other nuts

For raisin cake: ¾ cup chopped raisins

Preheat the oven to 325 degrees. Sift the baking powder and the flour together and set aside. In a large mixing bowl, mix together the butter and sugar. Add the eggs one at a time, beating well after each addition. Then add the lemon extract. Stir in half the flour followed by the milk and then the rest of the flour, beating well after each addition. Stir in the nuts or raisins, if desired. Pour the batter into three well-greased and floured mini loaf pans and bake until the cake is firm in the center and slightly pulled away from the sides, about 45 minutes.

NOTE: This recipe does make a lot of pound cake. You can make one of each kind by dividing the batter and adding just ¼ cup of nuts or raisins to one pan for each flavor. Well wrapped, the cake will keep for a week in the refrigerator or a month in the freezer.

"The wife complained to her husband that the chauffeur was very drunk indeed, and must be discharged instantly. "Discharged—nothing!" the husband retorted joyously. "When he's sobered off, I'll have him take me out and show me where he got it."

EDWARD J. CLODE, *JOKES FOR ALL OCCASIONS*

THE BARKEEPER'S DILEMMA

"Many are the readjustments which the coming of prohibition has brought to the industrial and commercial world. Perhaps the most serious problem . . . has been that of the ultimate fate of the breweries with their buildings and machine equipment representing an investment of $700,000,000 or more. The plight of the middle-aged person with flat feet and soft hands who knows how to do nothing except serve drinks and who is barred by legislative enactment from this occupation furnishes ample material for humor or tragedy, according to the resourcefulness of the individual." —Arthur L. Dahl, "What About Our Wine Grapes?" *Scientific American*, June 12, 1920

Royal Drop Cupcakes

4 tablespoons (¼ cup) butter
2 cups flour
1 cup sugar
1 teaspoon baking powder
1 egg
1 teaspoon vanilla extract
1 cup milk

Preheat the oven to 350 degrees. Line cupcake pans with paper liners or grease and flour. Melt the butter and set aside. Sift flour, sugar, and baking powder into a medium mixing bowl. In a separate bowl, stir the egg and vanilla into the milk. Pour these liquid ingredients along with the butter into the dry ingredients and stir with a spoon or spatula until blended. Fill cupcake cups about two-thirds full and bake until firm in the center, 20 to 25 minutes. Makes 12–14 regular-size cupcakes.

Variations: For orange use orange extract instead of vanilla; for spice add 2 teaspoons cinnamon.

Chocolate Cupcakes

4 tablespoons (¼ cup) butter
2 (1-ounce) squares unsweetened baking chocolate
2 cups flour
1 cup sugar
1 teaspoon baking powder
1 egg
1 teaspoon vanilla extract
1 cup milk

Preheat the oven to 350 degrees. Line cupcake pans with paper liners or grease and flour. Melt the butter and chocolate together and set aside. Sift flour, sugar, and baking powder into a medium mixing bowl. In a separate bowl, stir the egg and vanilla into the milk. Pour these liquid ingredients along with the butter and chocolate mixture into the dry ingredients and stir with a spoon or spatula until blended. Fill cupcake cups about two-thirds full and bake until firm in the center, 20 to 25 minutes. Makes 12–14 regular-size cupcakes.

ESTABLISHING A TRUSTED BOOTLEGGER

"We had a bootlegger in our town that the businessmen couldn't trust. We found him handling bad liquor. We just naturally had him arrested, and then we set up a young fellow in business that we could trust. He gets our liquor for us reasonably and we can depend on him. He turns his liquor over to the grocery man and the grocery's boy brings it. We all have regular standing orders with him." —E. E. Free, "Where America Gets Its Booze," *Popular Science,* May 1930

Coffee Raisin Cupcakes

1 cup raisins

2 cups plus 1 tablespoon flour

4 tablespoons (¼ cup) butter

1 teaspoon baking powder

1 cup firmly packed brown sugar

1 egg

1 teaspoon vanilla extract

½ cup milk

½ cup strong coffee

Preheat the oven to 350 degrees. Line cupcake pans with paper liners or grease and flour. Chop the raisins roughly into quarters and mix with 1 tablespoon flour. Set aside. Melt the butter and set aside. Sift 2 cups flour and baking powder into a medium mixing bowl; stir in brown sugar. In a separate bowl, stir the egg and vanilla into the milk and coffee. Pour these liquid ingredients along with the butter into the dry ingredients, including the raisins, and stir with a spoon or spatula until blended. Fill cupcake cups about two-thirds full and bake until firm in the center, 20 to 25 minutes. Makes 12–14 regular-size cupcakes.

THE PROHIBITION ERA COMES TO AN END

Mr. Fred Clark, President, The Young Crusaders of America, reflected on the organization's success:

"When we started this organization in 1922 Clarence Darrow told me that it was absolutely hopeless; we could never get two-thirds of the Senate to vote for repeal. Arthur Brisbane came out in his column and said the Young Crusaders have started to repeal the amendment.

"Mabel Walker Willebrandt [U.S. assistant attorney general for Prohibition enforcement] was coming through Cleveland. I had breakfast with her that morning. She said, 'Mr. Clark, take it from me, you will spend the rest of your life at this; it is absolutely futile.'

"So with all that encouragement, we started out. (Laughter) And we rolled up our membership pretty fast . . .

"There were Prohibitionists which consisted of a very small minority of the American public that put over the Eighteenth Amendment. Their purpose was sincere, they had a noble purpose, but it took us thirteen years to find out that their method of obtaining temperance in this country was not the right method. The only thing they succeeded in doing was taking this great industry out of legal hands and turning it over to the bootleggers and the gangsters, and making it five times more profitable."
—"Convention Banquet of the Psi Upsilon Fraternity," June 1934

An objector to prohibition spoke bitterly:
"Water has killed more folks than liquor ever did."
"You are raving," declared the defender of the
Eighteenth Amendment. "How do you make that out?"
"Well, to begin with, there was the Flood."

EDWARD J. CLODE, *JOKES FOR ALL OCCASIONS*

Tea Biscuits

2 cups flour
1 teaspoon baking powder
¼ teaspoon salt
1 tablespoon sugar
1 egg, lightly beaten
1 tablespoon butter, melted
½ cup water

Preheat the oven to 350 degrees. Sift flour, baking powder, salt, and sugar together into a medium mixing bowl. In a small bowl, add the egg and melted butter to the water, stir to combine, and then stir into the dry ingredients. Mix with a fork and then knead lightly for a minute or so until a smooth dough forms. Roll out on a floured board to about ½ inch thick. Cut with biscuit cutter. If you like, gently dip the top of the biscuits into some sugar. Place on a lightly greased baking sheet and bake until just turning brown on top, about 25 minutes. Makes 18 (1-inch) biscuits.

ACKNOWLEDGMENTS

These pages celebrate the American spirit of accomplishment and of seeing opportunity in unexpected situations. So I begin my acknowledgments by celebrating and thanking the archivists who collect, catalog, and make available original documents and those who create and maintain searchable, digital online archives. Through reading thousands of pages, both in person and online, I gained perspective and unexpected insights into this dynamic period.

In particular I am indebted to the Minnesota Historical Society and to reference specialist Debbie Miller, who knows the society's materials so well. Over the years that I have worked with those collections, Debbie has cheerfully and capably guided me to just the resource I need, whether I knew it or not when I asked the first question. Thank you, Debbie.

Keyword searches through Google Books and *New York Times* online archives brought forth wonderful first-person narratives, period analysis, and great recipes. My thanks to those whose efforts and investments have expanded the research possibilities for all of us.

I am indebted to those who carried my work on its journey from my desktop. Percolator Graphic Design and photographer Brian Gardner put my words and recipes inside this beautiful cover. My deepest thanks, too, to the team gathered at Minnesota Historical Society Press. It is my great pleasure to work with director Pam McClanahan and the rest of this wonderful group: Ann Regan, Dan Leary, Mary Poggione, Alison Aten, Leslie Rask, and incomparable editor Shannon Pennefeather.

And, always, my thanks to John for everything.

Notes

NOTES TO INTRODUCTION

1. *National Druggist*, February 1920, 92.
2. *The Soda Fountain*, October 1921, 32.
3. *The Soda Fountain*, January 1921, 37.
4. *Northwest Druggist*, February 1921, 50.
5. Menus from the collection of the Minnesota Historical Society.
6. *The Soda Fountain*, January 1921, 37.

NOTES TO "BREWERIES AND MAIN STREETS FIND SALVATION IN ICE CREAM"

1. Mullendore, *History of the United States Food Administration*, 109.
2. "House, 176 to 55, Overrides Veto of War Prohibition," *New York Times*, October 28, 1919.
3. Mabel Willebrandt, "How Wet Is Dry America," *New York Times*, August 7, 1929.
4. Historic American Engineering Report prepared by the Rocky Mountain Park Service, Department of the Interior, n.d., received from the Morrison County Historical Society; "Two Modern Plants," *Little Falls Daily Transcript*, November 3, 1913.
5. "Milk and Cream Products Plant," *Little Falls Daily Transcript*, January 20, 1920.
6. "Kiewels Open Plant Today," *Little Falls Daily Transcript*, August 31, 1933; "Brewery to be Made Larger," *Little Falls Daily Transcript*, May 2, 1934.
7. *The Expositor* 21 (1919–20); *The International Confectioner* (September 1919): 79.
8. *Current Opinion* 68.4 (April 1920): 457.

9. *Current Opinion* 68.4 (April 1920): 457.
10. Anti-Saloon League Museum, http://www .wpl.lib.oh.us/AntiSaloon/history/ (accessed February 20, 2013).
11. "Wayne Wheeler," Anti-Saloon League Museum, http://www.wpl.lib.oh.us/AntiSaloon /leaders/wayne_wheeler/ (accessed February 20, 2013).
12. "Printed Materials," Anti-Saloon League Museum, http://www.wpl.lib.oh.us/AntiSaloon /pmaterial/fliers/ (accessed February 20, 1913).
13. Okrent, *Last Call*, 29–30; Smith, *The Sober World*, 398.
14. "Experience in Grand Rapids May be Typical," *The Continent*, February 21, 1919, 244; *Anti-Saloon League Yearbook* (1920).
15. Hernon and Ganey, *Under the Influence*, 134.
16. *The Expositor and Current Anecdotes* 21 (June 1920): 905.

NOTES TO "THE PRICE PAID BY ANDREW VOLSTEAD"

1. "House Overrides Prohibition Veto," *New York Times*, October 28, 1919.
2. "Sees Long Delay in Lifting Ban," *New York Times*, July 1, 1919.
3. "Volstead Wins Nomination on Kvale's Atheist Charges," *New York Times*, July 21, 1920.
4. "Court Rejects Both Volstead and Kvale," *New York Times*, September 11, 1920.
5. "Volstead Scores Tinkham," *New York Times*, June 24, 1922.
6. June 3, 1921, box 2, Volstead Papers, Minnesota Historical Society, St. Paul.

7. Diggins, Mo., June 5, 1922, box 2, Volstead Papers, Minnesota Historical Society, St. Paul.

8. Balto, April 19, 1921, box 1, Volstead Papers, Minnesota Historical Society, St. Paul.

9. "Unclubby Mr. Volstead," *New York Times,* August 6, 1921.

10. "Verbal Assault Voted by the House 181 to 2," *New York Times,* August 25, 1921; "Reed Strikes Out Fling at Volstead," *New York Times,* November 24, 1921.

11. "House Hoots Down Attack on Volstead," *New York Times,* August 25, 1922.

12. *New York Times,* November 8, 1933.

NOTES TO "OPPORTUNISTS, SCOFFLAWS, AND BOOTLEGGERS"

1. Okrent, *Last Call,* 56; http://en.wikipedia .org/wiki/Income_tax_in_the_United _States#Ratification_of_the_Sixteenth _Amendment, accessed February 17, 2013.

2. "Kramer Sums Up First Dry Year," *New York Times,* January 16, 1921; "Kramer on Prohibition Problems," *The N.A.R.D. [National Association of Retail Druggists] Journal,* June 23, 1921, 480.

3. Letter, L. C. Quinn, *The Mixer and Server,* March 15, 1922, 21; Merz, *The Dry Decade,* 277, 332–33.

4. Merz, *The Dry Decade,* 127.

5. "Can Prohibition be Made Effective?" *New York Times,* August 25, 1929.

6. Merz, *The Dry Decade,* 129.

7. "House Drys Rule Prohibition Fight," *New York Times,* July 20, 1919.

8. "Allow Home Brew Over Half Per Cent," *New York Times,* June 24, 1920.

9. "New Grape Syrup Industry," *The Soda Fountain* (March 1921): 27; "Development of the Grape Syrup Industry," *The Soda Fountain* (March 1921): 29; Okrent, *Last Call,* 335.

10. John Walker Harrington, "Measuring the Home-Brew Kick," *Popular Science Monthly* 98 (January 1921): 44.

11. Fabian Franklin, *What Prohibition Has Done to America,* 19; "How Wet Is Dry America," *New York Times,* August 7, 1929; E. E. Free, "Where America Gets Its Booze," *Popular Science*

(May 1930): 137; Kyvig, "Sober Thoughts: Myths and Realities of National Prohibition after Fifty Years," in Kyvig, *Law, Alcohol, and Order,* 13.

12. *New York Times,* November 24, 1929.

13. Okrent, *Last Call,* 361.

NOTES TO "SUFFRAGISTS, SALOONS, AND SODA SHOPS"

1. Available: http://www.poemhunter.com /poem/come-home-father/ (accessed November 8, 2012).

2. L. Ames Brown, "Prohibition and Suffrage," *North American Review* 203.1 (January 1916): 93–100; Taft quoted in Joseph V. McKee, A.M., "Shall Women Vote?" *Catholic World* (October 1915): 51.

3. L. Ames Brown, "Suffrage and Prohibition," *The North American Review* 203.1 (January 1916): 95.

4. Speech, December 8, 1921, box 4, Volstead Papers, Minnesota Historical Society, St. Paul.

5. "Catering to Women Patrons," *The Soda Fountain* (January 1921): 26.

6. Russell Owen, "Saloon to Speakeasy," *New York Times,* January 22, 1933.

7. Sabin quoted in Okrent, *Last Call,* 224; "Mrs. Sabin to Survey Effects of Dry Law Among Wives of Workers Throughout the Nation," *New York Times,* July 2, 1929.

8. "Mrs. Sabin Proposes a 'Party Moratorium,'" *New York Times,* January 1, 1932.

9. Russell Owen, "Saloon to Speakeasy," *New York Times,* January 22, 1933.

NOTES TO "MODERN ENTERTAINMENT BUILDS SODA BUSINESS"

1. Walrus manufacturing company ad, "Do not be extravagant by being economical," *The Practical Druggist* (December 1921): 49.

2. "Important Information from Advertisers," "Great Changes in the Soda Business," *National Association of Retail Druggists Journal,* April 17, 1919, 95.

3. "$1,000,000,000 for Soda," *New York Times,* May 14, 1922.

4. "Telling Tips," *Midland Druggist and Pharmaceutical Review* (August 1921): 289.

5. Broadcasting stations alphabetically by name from *Commercial and Government Radio Stations of the United States* (Washington, DC: U.S. Government Printing Office, 1922), 70–72, available: http://earlyradiohistory.us/220630ci.htm (accessed October 31, 2012), and Eric Barnow, *A Tower in Babel: A History of Broadcasting in the United States to 1933* (New York: Oxford University Press, 1966), 79.

6. Frank Marston, "Have the First Radio Station in Town at Your Store," *Candy and Soda Fountain Profits* (June 1922): 5.

7. Barnow, *A Tower in Babel*, 79, 145.

8. Russell Owen, "Saloon to Speakeasy," *New York Times*, January 22, 1933.

9. *Midland Druggist and Pharmaceutical Review (Interstate Druggist)* (August 1921): 291.

NOTES TO "ON THE ROAD"

1. Lawrence William Pedrose, "Motorists' Caravansary is New Industry," *Popular Mechanics* (October 1922): 523.

2. Katherine Lafitte, "Burning Gas on the Gypsy Trail," *Outing* (April 1922): 298.

3. Pedrose, "Motorists' Caravansary," 523; A. L. Buzzell, ed., *The Bulletin of Pharmacy* (1921): 371.

4. *The Soda Fountain* (May 1921): 30.

NOTES TO "NO FREE LUNCH"

1. "Drink Prices Go Up, Abolish Free Lunch," *New York Times*, July 11, 1917.

2. Raymond Calkins, *Substitutes for the Saloon* (Boston: Houghton Mifflin Company, 1919), 16–18.

3. "Drink Prices Go Up; Abolish Free Lunch," *New York Times*, July 11, 1917.

4. "Now the Luncheonette," *The Gas Record*, April 14, 1920, 25.

5. Rev. Charles Stelzle, "The Old Saloon," letter to the editor, *New York Times*, September 9, 22, 1932.

6. "1,000,000 Men Need Saloon Substitute," *New York Times*, December 15, 1918.

7. "Has Prohibition Been a Benefit to the Workingmen and Their Families?" *The Mixer and Server*, November 15, 1920, 38.

8. Gompers to Benjamin Johnson, February 24, 1917, in *Cigarmakers Official Journal* (April 1917): 11, quoted in Nuala McGan Drescher, "Labor and Prohibition: The Unappreciated Impact of the Eighteenth Amendment," in ed. David E. Kyvig, *Law, Alcohol, and Order Perspectives on National Prohibition*, Contributions in American History 110 (Westport, CT: Greenwood Press, 1985), 36.

9. Gompers testimony, *Prohibiting Intoxicating Beverages*, Hearings before United States Senate Subcommittee on the Judiciary, June 14, 1919, 9–10, available from Google Books.

10. Gompers testimony, 11.

11. "Women Aid a Saloon Substitute," *New York Times*, April 4, 1920; "Anti-Saloon Head Assails Carstensen," *New York Times*, February 26, 1926.

12. Stelzle, "The Old Saloon."

NOTES TO "LIGHT AND SPECIALIZED MEALS

1. *The Soda Fountain* (March 1921): 23.

2. *Northwestern Druggist* (February 1922): 58.

Bibliography

Asterisks indicate sources for recipes.

BOOKS

*Apell, Charles. *Up-to-Date Candy Teacher.* Bloomington, IL: The author, 1921.

Barnow, Erik. *A Tower in Babel: A History of Broadcasting in the United States to 1933.* New York: Oxford University Press, 1966.

Beman, Lamar T., comp. *Selected Articles on Prohibition: Modification of the Volstead Law.* New York: H. W. Wilson Company, 1924.

*Board of Directors, comp. *Castelar Creche Cook Book.* Los Angeles: Times-Mirror Printing and Binding, 1922.

Calkins, Raymond. *Substitutes for the Saloon.* 2nd ed., revised. Boston: Houghton Mifflin Company, 1919.

Cherrington, Ernest Hurst, ed. *Anti-Saloon League Yearbook.* Waterville, OH: Anti-Saloon League, 1920.

Clode, Edward. *Jokes for All Occasions.* New York: Edward Clode, 1921, 1922.

Collegiate World Publishing. *College Humor, 1920–1921.* Chicago: The company, 1921.

Drescher, Nuala McGan. "Labor and Prohibition: The Unappreciated Impact of the Eighteenth Amendment." In *Kyvig, Law, Alcohol, and Order.*

*Editorial Staff of *The Soda Fountain. The Dispenser's Formulary, or Soda Water Guide.* New York: D. O. Haynes and Company, 1915.

*Geographical Publishing Company, comp. *Twentieth Century Cook Book.* Chicago: The company, 1921.

Hernon, Peter, and Terry Ganey. *Under the Influence: The Unauthorized Story of the Anheuser-Busch Dynasty.* New York: Simon and Schuster, 1991.

Herrick, Frank. E. *Prohibition Poems and Other Verse.* Elgin, IL: Brethern Publishing, 1914.

Kahn, Alexander. *A Prohibition Primer.* New York: John Day, 1931.

*Kahnweiler, Bert. *Common Sense Drug Store Advertising.* New York: The author, 1921.

Kobler, John. *Ardent Spirits.* New York: G. P. Putnam's Sons, 1973.

Kyvig, David E., ed. *Law, Alcohol, and Order: Perspectives on National Prohibition.* Contributions in American History 110. Westport, CT: Greenwood Press, 1985.

Leacock, Stephen. *Wet Wit and Dry Humor.* New York: Dodd, Mead and Company, Inc., 1931.

Lewis, Sinclair. *Main Street.* New York: Harcourt, Brace and Company, 1921.

McEvoy, J. P. *The Sweet Dry and Dry.* Chicago: P. E. Volland Company, 1919.

Merz, Charles. *The Dry Decade.* Seattle: University of Washington Press, 1931.

Mullendore, William C. *History of the United States Food Administration, 1917–1919.* Stanford, CA: Stanford University Press, 1941.

Neal, Robert Wilson. *Editorials and Editorial Writing.* New York: Home Correspondence School, Inc., 1921.

Okrent, Daniel. *Last Call: The Rise and Fall of Prohibition.* New York: Scribner, 2010.

*Richards, Lenore, and Nola Treat. *Tea Room Recipes.* Boston: Little, Brown and Company, 1925.

*Rigby, W. O., and Fred Rigby. *Rigby's Reliable Candy Teacher.* Topeka, KS: Rigby Publishing Company, 1920.

Rogers, Will. *The Cowboy Philosopher on Prohibition.* New York: Harper and Brothers, 1919.

Schoenberg, Robert J. *Mr. Capone.* New York: Harper Collins, 1993.

Smith, Randolph Wellford. *The Sober World.*

Boston: Marshall Jones Company, 1919.

Taylor, Henry C. *After the Town Goes Dry*. Chicago: Howell Publishing Company, 1919.

U.S. Congress Committee on the Judiciary. *Prohibiting Intoxicating Beverages*. Vol. 1–3. Hearings before the Subcommittee. July 8, 1919. Reprint: Memphis, TN: General Books LLC.

*Whitehead, Jessup. *Cooking for Profit*. Chicago: Jessup Whitehead and Co., 1893.

Willebrandt, Mabel. *The Inside of Prohibition*. Indianapolis: Bobbs-Merrill Company, 1929.

NEWSPAPERS AND MAGAZINES

American Cookery, formerly the *Boston Cooking School Magazine* (1921–22)

American Druggist and Pharmaceutical Record (1919)

The American Magazine

Bulletin of Pharmacy

Candy and Soda Profits (1921, 1922)

Catholic World

Collier's

Confectioners' and Bakers' Gazette (1919, 1922)

Cosmopolitan

Current Opinion

Delineator (1925)

The Diamond of Psi Upsilon

The Druggist Circular (1919)

The Expositor

The Gas Record

Ice and Refrigeration

The International Confectioner (1919)

Life and Labor Bulletin

Little Falls Daily Transcript

Midland Druggist and Pharmaceutical Review (1921)

The Mixer and Server

National Association of Retail Druggist Journal

The New York Times

North American Review

Northwest Druggist (1921, 1922)

Northwestern Druggist (1922)

Outing

The Outlook

Popular Mechanics

Popular Science

Practical Druggist and Pharmaceutical Review of Reviews (1921)

Prairie Farmer (1888)

Printer's Ink

The Rotarian

Saturday Evening Post

Scientific American

The Soda Fountain (1921, 1922)

The Spatula (1921, 1922)

The Textile Worker

COLLECTIONS

Andrew J. Volstead Papers. Minnesota Historical Society, St. Paul.

Kiewel Brewing Company Collection. Morrison County Historical Society, Little Falls, MN.

Recipe Index

Subject Index